Woodturning

in pictures

Woodturning

in pictures Bruce Boulter

Sterling Publishing Co., Inc. New York

Published in 1983 by Sterling Publishing Co., Inc.
Two Park Avenue, New York, N.Y. 10016

Filmset in 11/12 pt Plantin and printed in Great Britain
by BAS Printers Limited, Over Wallop, Hampshire.

ISBN 0–8069–5492–2 (Trade)
ISBN 0–8069–7742–6 (Paperback)

Published by arrangement with Bell & Hyman Ltd.
This edition available in the United States, Canada and the Philippine
Islands only.

Contents

Introduction

Woodturning is a craft which anyone with any practical aptitude can learn. The methods described in this book are based on those learned in my apprenticeship over thirty years ago, updated and modified to accommodate modern equipment. I would not, however, insist that my ways are the only ways and would encourage any turner to experiment.

I have not started with a chapter on lathes. Every lathe has its merits and in the light of the text the turner can assess and adapt the methods described. Nor do I believe there is a basic set of tools. This depends on the type of turning to be done and I have always been a believer in the approach that one doesn't sharpen a tool until it is needed and doesn't buy a tool until you need to sharpen it. The tools and accessories will be discussed as they are used and at each stage their usefulness will be covered in detail.

As a young apprentice my first chance at the lathe was to help in the making of several thousand banister posts. After the first few hundred I was quite good at making them! Another early job was to turn over a hundred newel posts in oak. The stuff was 20cm (8in) square and (5ft 6in) long; I am now quite undaunted by the size of any timber on the lathe but I must admit that when the first of those newel posts started whizzing around it was a minute or three before I could summon up the courage to approach it. I mention this bit of history to emphasise the need for practice and confidence. With the right tool, properly prepared, in your hand and the guidance I trust this book will provide, woodturning will give you many hours, and indeed years, of satisfaction and pleasure.

I have discovered from the pupils I teach that the necessity for tool preparation is in no way appreciated. It gives me great pleasure to show them that there is no secret in preparation and as one of them said to me recently, 'you know, it is much more simple to do it the right way'. As a result, the first chapters concentrate on the tools and equipment required to prepare turning tools. This is followed by chapters on the different types of turning giving an introduction to the tools that will be required and an indication of the angles to which they should be prepared. I doubt that too much variation from the suggestions given will be necessary but at the same time would encourage experiment when working with different timbers.

Finally, various projects are described to amplify the tool use described in the earlier chapters and to demonstrate my approach to making turned objects. At all times I have indicated lathe speeds which should give the best results. Speeds in turning are very much like bevel angles, a lot will depend on personal preference as experience grows but I would suggest always starting slow and speed up if necessary rather than the other way round. For the same reason I have not specified exact tool rest heights although the photographs will give guidance. The photographs have been taken from both sides of the lathe and from both ends to give as clear a view as possible. The terms left and right in the text, however, always refer to the working position, as the turner would see the work.

Finally, I have drawn attention at various times to the need for safety when working with any machine tool but for fear of misleading or giving the reader the impression that woodturning is a dangerous occupation, which it certainly is not, I have not over-emphasised the subject. I would, however, be completely failing in my duty if I did not bring to the readers attention the fact that dangers are inherent when using machinery of any type, but with care, attention to the makers instructions, placement of protective guards, and in no circumstances making any modifications to these guards, there is no greater danger than crossing a road provided the correct procedures are followed. While it is quite impossible for me to cover every eventuality I would like to draw attention to the practice of making turning tools from worn-out files. There are many types and qualities of steel and they all have their uses, the steel used in the production of files is suitable for files, it is *not* suitable for woodworking tools and may be hazardous. It is also quite unnecessary as blank tools can be purchased in the correct grade of steel and special shapes can be made from these with ease, and with the assurance that the product has been produced by toolmakers who know what they are doing. So, make safety in the workshop as important as producing fine work, stop and reflect often, and with a calm and inquisitive approach enjoy your woodturning.

The electric grindstone

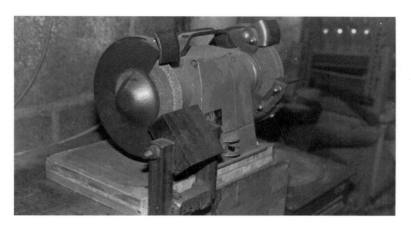

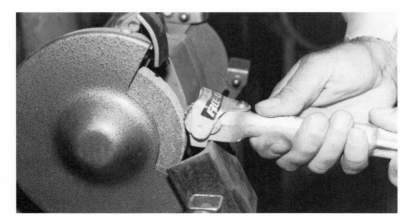

Fig. 1.   The ideal grinder for the woodturner is the electric type, double-ended with one wheel of fine grit No. 80 P6V and one of coarse grit No. 36 WU6B.

The fine wheel is used for scrapers and is fine enough to produce a finish to the tool so that it may be used straight from the grinder. The coarse wheel is fast cutting and will not, therefore, cause any unnecessary heat build-up, and as we will be honing all cutting tools before use this wheel will be used to give shape only.

The wheels of electric grinders are cutting tools in their own right and must be treated with care and attention. In use the wheels become clogged with tiny particles of steel and if left untreated will appear glazed or polished. They should never be allowed to reach this state, as this will render them blunt and a great deal of pressure will be required by the operator to effect any cutting action, and in extreme cases the wheel will not cut at all.

Fig. 2.   The wheels are kept clean (open) and in top condition with a tool called a wheel dresser.

Fig. 3.   The small spiked wheels, separated by steel washers, are offered gently to the revolving emery wheel in a stroking movement across the face. The wheel dresser will revolve at a greater speed and will produce a scouring action on the face of the emery wheel, cutting away the glaze and rendering a new cutting face. The spike wheels and washers are replaceable for this type of dresser and it is, I think, to be preferred to the carborundum type.

This is a dusty job and, until you get used to it, a little fearsome and noisy, but it is necessary and not the least bit dangerous. That being said the grinder can, like any other machine tool, inflict serious injury but care and concentration will go a long way in avoiding accidents. Never operate the grinder without eye protection, and preferably full-face protection.

Fig. 4.   A selection of safety masks.

Never grind on the side of a power-driven emery wheel, it is not designed for the purpose, is not stressed to take the sideways pressure and for woodturning tools this is quite unnecessary and added to that it cannot be dressed nor should any attempt be made to do so if you have been using the side. Never use one that is not *completely* guarded *all round* by the manufacturer's guards. Do not modify them or remove them, other than to change or inspect a wheel and then replace at once.

Never mount an unguarded wheel on the out-board end of the lathe as this is a vulnerable position and the wheel may be struck without your knowledge. Such a blow could crack the wheel and when the lathe is started, or you come to use it, it will shatter with disastrous consequences. Remember an emery wheel looks almost the same running or stationary so switch it off when not in use.

Never, in any circumstances, attempt to make your own grinder from old or discarded domestic appliance motors, such motors will run at speeds too high or too low for the purpose, and can be most dangerous. A tragic death was reported recently when a home-made grinder travelling at a speed of 22,000 rpm, shattered the wheel and killed the operator. Emery wheels are recommended to work at spindle speeds of plus or minus 5,000 rpm, unless otherwise specified. Never leave a grinder running unattended, and cover it to keep it free from dust when not in use.

It is good policy to remove the wheel at intervals, thread it on a screwdriver through the spindle hole and hold it close to your ear. Flick it with a fingernail, not a hammer, and it will emit a clear ring if it is sound and not cracked, if it does not after a few flicks discard it at once. This test can also be used when buying a new wheel, and the shopkeeper will respect your diligence, if he does not, shop elsewhere. For greater detail on safety consult industrial regulations for machine tools in general.

Oilstones and whetstones

Fig. 5. A selection of stones, qualities, and shapes.
The perfect cutting edge is one that has the minimum of
sawtooth effect. It follows, therefore, that the finer the
medium used to achieve the final edge the keener it will be.
With the knowledge of what is available and in the light of
the section on honing it will be a simple matter for you to
decide how far you wish to take it.

The most economical range of honing stones is the well-
known Carborundum, or India, both are man-made, the
former from carborundum, and the latter aloxite powders
bonded together, and will be found to be of a continuous
standard. These stones are available in a wide range of
shapes and sizes, and in various grits from coarse to fine,
and will give an excellent edge to all tools.

In the economy range of natural stones is Welsh slate.
I am not personally familiar with it, but I know those who
use it are pleased with the results.

Scotch Dalmore Fine Hone which I have never been able
to find out whether it is natural or man made, is another
economical stone. I have a couple and find them clean and
quick cutting.

At the other end of the scale come the very expensive but
superb natural stones, Washita and Arkansas. Both come
from the same place Hot Springs, Arkansas, U.S.A. The
state is, as I am sure you know pronounced ar-can-saw, the
stone a-can-sas. I am advised that Washita, is no longer

available so will not pursue the quality, but describe the
three grades of Arkansas. These stones are produced from a
natural volcanic rock called novaculite, which is, in effect,
pure silica.

The softest, coarsest and cheapest is Soft Arkansas. It is,
nevertheless, much finer, and will produce a keener edge,
than the finest man-made stone. It is recognised by its
blue/grey colour and a marble-like figure.

Next finest is White Arkansas which is a plain grey/white
colour sometimes with very fine yellowish lines, and is used
after the Soft Arkansas to further fine an edge.

Finally, Surgical or Black Arkansas which is very dark
grey, grey/black or black. This is the hardest of all and is
used to polish an edge that has been honed with White
Arkansas. Purchase stones from a reputable dealer, Hiram
Smith is one of the most well-known quarries. Nearly all
these stones will be found to have slight flaws which will in
no way impair the quality but stones with heavy or deep
pits and strong yellow lines (quartz lines) should be
refused, such are known as 'chit-chat' in the quarries. The
stones are very expensive but will last a lifetime or more
and give an edge to tools that cannot be bettered. Oil is the
lubricant for all the aforementioned except Welsh slate for
which water is recommended. Use a fine oil (3-in-1) to
lubricate, or one of the honing fluids advertised, and do not
ever soak any stone in oil.

As with the grinder, oilstones will become clogged in use
and must be kept clean. This is easily done by an overnight
soak in paraffin, followed by a scrub with an old brush or
toothbrush, then for the finer stones a wash in warm
detergent water will keep them in first-class cutting
condition. Keep them in boxes out of the working dust, and
to prevent the small ones, the slips, being swept up with the
shavings.

Stones that become hollow or mis-shapen in use can easily
be restored to their original shape as follows. Take a piece
of 6mm ($\frac{1}{4}$in) plate glass approximately 150mm × 300mm
(6in × 12in) in size and sprinkle some emery powder over it,
a little paraffin to moisten and lubricate and then work the
damaged section of the stone over this mixture. The stone
will soon be as good as new. If emery powder is not

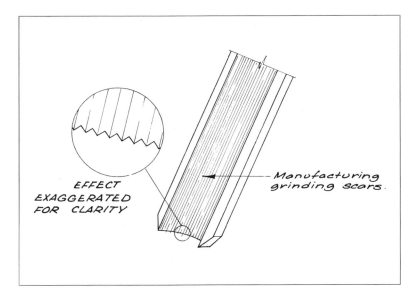

EFFECT EXAGGERATED FOR CLARITY

Manufacturing grinding scars.

available use valve-grinding paste well-diluted with paraffin. It is much the same thing and is available from motor accessory shops.

Your grinder and your honing stones are every bit as important as your finest tools or other equipment, care for them and they will repay their cost a thousandfold.

The perfect cutting edge.
It is common knowledge that a cutting edge is produced by abrading two adjacent surfaces, such abrasion will reduce the material being worked upon to a point of infinity, namely the edge. It has, however, been my experience that even folk who have been working in wood for many years do not really understand the principles involved, I have, therefore, used a bench plane iron for the purpose of demonstration as it is big and flat enough to illustrate well. The following will, of course, apply to all woodworking tools which after honing will be de-burred or backed off. The exceptions are parting tools and turners' chisels, that being said the principle will still be valid for all.

Fig. 6.   Shows a new iron as it would be purchased, ground by the makers to the correct angle for general purpose use. All you have to do is to hone it in the usual way and the edge so produced on the back of the tool, worked to infinity, is the cutting edge. But consider, is it really much of a cutting edge? In the normal course of manufacture the iron will have machining marks and/or scores all round and the finite edge will be so scored that it cannot possibly take anything like a keen edge. It will look, with very little magnification, like a saw. In fact in very severe cases if you draw your thumb nail along such an edge you may be able to feel the coarseness. It follows then that the part of any tool that is taking the edge must be smooth and flat, and with any new tool I proceed as follows.

Take a medium or coarse man-made oilstone and using

plenty of 3-in-1 or honing fluid, keep the iron dead flat on the stone. Use the full length and width of the stone, thus not dubbing the tool edge and maintaining the profile of the stone, and work away until satisfied that the deepest machining marks are removed. Then transfer to a Dalmore stone and spend a little time repeating the process to further reduce the roughness occasioned by the coarse man-made stone. Then to the Soft Arkansas and the difference between the area worked upon, and the rest of the back of the tool, can now be clearly seen. You could say that at this stage the tool is ready to take a keen edge, if honed in the normal way with a soft Arkansas thus putting an end to this dismal job! It is, of course, for you to decide, but permit me to take the process a stage further.

In Fig. 7 the iron on the left has been given the treatment as described above progressing from the Soft to the White Arkansas, and I concede that for all practical purposes this is as far as is necessary, in fact for gouges it will be as far as you will be able to take it as the slips required to effect the work on the *insides* of gouges are not available in Black Arkansas. If you study the iron on the right of Fig. 7 it will be clear from the reflection how polished the back of this iron is, and it will be equally obvious that when the hone is worked to the same degree a perfect cutting edge will result. This polish was produced with a Black Arkansas; in all it took about twenty minutes and as it will only be necessary to do all this work *once* in the life of the tool I do not consider this to be time wasted if it gives me a tool that will work to perfection right from the start. You will hear it said, indeed you may well have found, that tools seem to take a better edge as they grow older, and this is, of course, the reason for it. In the normal course of use, and with constant de-burring, the back becomes progressively more smooth, thus taking a continuously finer edge, that is if you are prepared to wait!

Fig. 8. Shows a roughing-out gouge set up to give it the inside polishing treatment; the process is exactly the same as previously described. The tang of the tool is cramped to the bench with some newspaper under it, and further held secure with a holdfast. Thus I can use two hands on the coarse stone to bring down the pressure required to flatten quickly which is sometimes necessary for tools that are beaten into shape as is the roughing-out gouge. Once flat and reasonably smooth the rest of the fining process will only take a few moments. A little paraffin used as well as lubricating oil will help to speed the process. It is not necessary to have a stone to fit all sizes of gouge as long as it will fit inside and reach the base. All that will be required will be to push with the stone to one side and pull it back on the opposite side on the alternate stroke. I like to treat all gouges in the same manner, i.e. spindle as well as the roughing-out gouge. Take care not to dub the end, see Fig. 16 and 17, and take extra care with the new types of gouge such as the superflute or high-speed steel tools that are now available. These are excellent tools and well worth the investment, but the flute in them is not as long as in the normal tool, in addition it is a machined shape and as the handle end of the flute rises gently it will encourage the stone to tip downwards at the cutting edge, and this *must* be avoided.

Grinding the bevel
Now that the tools are prepared inside to whatever degree you wish to take the process, we can turn our attention to grinding an accurate and continuous bevel which is of such a shape that it will make honing a quick and simple matter.

Fig. 9. Years ago I prepared a rest for beginners that is strong, robust and, most important, completely accurate. You can, of course, use the rests that are provided with the grinder, but experience has shown me that these are usually too small, and being supported on one side only on most grinders, permit a slight flexibility in use. If you can make your own, or have one made, you will find it a great help.

Fig. 10. A similar rest that can be made in the workshop, albeit three or more will be required to accommodate the various angles of grind that will be necessary. They are of the quick release type, so it is a simple matter to change from one angle to another. With either of these rests it will be found that the tool can be rested on and passed round the face of the wheel without any pressure thus keeping heat build-up to a minimum. Quench the tool to keep it completely cold, inspect, and replace it for successive passes. The tool will be at *exactly* the same angle which eliminates the temptation to apply heavy pressure to effect the grind in one pass and the fear of burning the tool in the process. It will also effect a hollow grind to the ground area and this makes the honing fool-proof, and also extends the life of the tool considerably. The first tool used for between centres work will be the roughing-out gouge, which I feel is an inappropriately named tool as the word 'roughing' indicates a tool for rough work. This is far from true as this is a tool that is capable of fine work, and in situations of awkward or interlocking grain, working through knots, etc., it will sometimes be found that this is the only tool that will give a fine finish. So let us discuss its preparation, starting with grinding.

Fig. 11. With the rest prepared to render a ground angle on the tool of approximately 45° (two or three degrees either way will make little difference) place the fingers of the left hand under some convenient part of the rest (take care not to foul the wheel), bring the thumb down on the tool in a pinching action that will ensure the tool is held *flat* on the rest all the way round the grind.

Fig. 12. With the tool handle supported against the leg, the right hand, kept well up to the rest for complete control, is used to revolve the tool and to keep it in line with the rotation of the wheel, right round the tool from tip to tip.

Fig. 13. The finish position. It is important to effect this process from tip to tip, as if this is not done it will result in an overground U-base with two horns at the tips of the U which must be avoided. Try a few dry runs with the grinder switched off to get the feel of the movement. Now switch on, take your time, place the tool on its side on the prepared rest clear of the wheel and advance it to contact, very gently. It is, of course, possible to start on either side and, in fact, alternating the movement is a good idea, so that if there is a slight tendency to apply a little more pressure at one point, the reverse pass will eliminate it. With the gentle pressure you have applied the tool should be quite cool but place it in the quench pot, anyway, to avoid any build up of heat; inspect and repeat for as many more passes as are deemed necessary. You will now see that subsequent passes will not have altered the angle in any

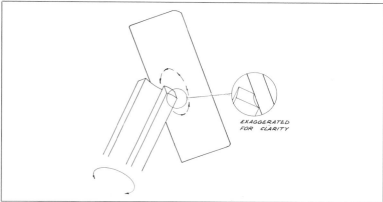

EXAGGERATED
FOR CLARITY

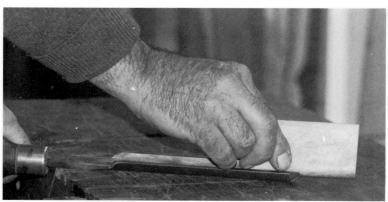

way. If necessary you may have to grind right up to the tip of the tool to establish this angle, if so take great care as the steel at the tip is very thin and will burn. Using the recommended coarse wheel you won't find this too much of a problem and this will be the only time you will have to grind right up to the end. With the recommended size wheel of 127–152mm (5–6in) diameter you will have an accurate and continuous grind that will, by virtue of the diameter of wheel, be hollow ground.

Honing

Fig. 14.   Prop the tool up on some convenient and firm place in the workshop. The stone is held and maintained in the position shown.

Fig. 15.   Shown here exaggerated for clarity. The stone bridges the two sides of the hollow grind and the tool is revolved through its own axis while the stone is revolved as per the arrows. Work all round the tool with a coarse stone to remove the saw effect that will have been produced by the coarse wheel, then finish with your finest stone. Note: it is a waste of time to hone with a stone that is finer than that with which the inside of the tool will be de-burred. Honed this way it will be impossible to round the tool as you will have two distinct points to guide the stone. With successive honing the two high points will diminish and the ground area will become flat. Just before this stage is reached it will be time to re-grind. If, in the meantime, the rest has been altered to grind another tool to a different angle use the gouge as a guide (the honing will not have altered its angle) to re-set the rest and proceed as before. Do *not* grind right up to the tip of the tool, just grind enough to re-establish the hollow shape and stop before the grinding goes right up to the tool edge. It will now be obvious that while all this seems a lot of work it does save not only time and tool steel, but the edge that you have so carefully prepared with, say, a White Arkansas will never be disturbed. Even after re-grinding it will only be necessary to work up the edge with the White Arkansas or your finest stone. I have stressed this to some extent, but as it will apply to *all* tools it will not be necessary to go through the theory with each tool.

Fig. 16.   To start de-burring, hold the stone at the *rear* and push forward.

Fig. 17.   Stop before the fingers pass the end and draw back. In this way there will be no fear of dubbing as the weight of the hand is on the tool at all times and never passes the end. Take care in both honing and de-burring, the tool is now very sharp and can nip the tips of the fingers off almost without you knowing!

Making a start

Let us now put this tool to use. I have chosen for the purpose of demonstration a length of stuff 10cm (4in) square. It may seem a daunting size in the square, but I assure you it is not in the least bit difficult or dangerous. Do not take the corners off first with a plane. Surely that is what you bought the lathe for, and if you get into the habit what happens when you want to work a table leg or similar that requires square ends? Two exceptions would be if the stuff was a rare or valuable timber, in which case the corners could be removed on the saw table and the waste kept for some other use, sandglass columns, lace bobbins, etc.; or if the size of the stuff was such that with the corners on it would not clear the lathe bed.

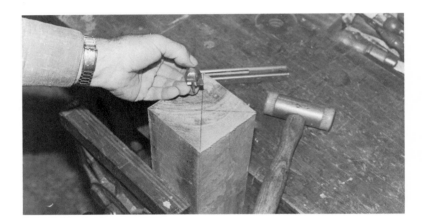

Fig. 18. Find the centre by marking across the diagonals and take a drive centre, preferably with four spurs and tap it in with a soft or plastic-faced hammer. If this is not possible because the timber is particularly hard, saw a kerf across the marked diagonals and drill a hole for the centre.

Fig. 19. Tap the drive centre well into the timber.

Fig. 20. With a drill or awl make a small hole the other end to accept the tailstock centre.

Fig. 21.   A revolving or live centre, so called because it will turn with the work and will, therefore, require only the minimum of attention while working.

Fig. 22.   A dead centre, it enters the work in the same way as the live but is fixed and will require lubrication; linseed oil used sparingly to avoid unnecessary marking of the work is ideal, alternatively use candle (paraffin) wax but *not* lubricating oil (motor oil or 3-in-1) as it will stain.

Fig. 23.   A ring or cup centre is also fixed and will require lubricating. Its shape makes it most useful for work that is subject to splitting, for split turning and for long hole boring.

All three are supported by a morse taper to the tailstock which on most lathes will be self-ejecting. There is also on the market a revolving centre that will accommodate all three of these different shapes or methods. It is described in use on page 66. The height of the lathe is important. It should be sited so that the line between centres, is approximately 25mm (1in) below elbow height of the user. This ensures comfort and ease of use and it will never be necessary to stoop or over reach. Ideally the lathe stand should be bolted to the floor or at the very least weighted with bricks, etc. to dampen any vibration that may occur.

With the stuff secured in the lathe tighten the tailstock. Do not overtighten as this will occasion unnecessary wear on the bearings and, if you are using a dead centre, some smoke and a screeching noise.

Fig. 24.   Set the tool rest low for working down to a cylinder. Notice that the corners of the stuff will come down on the cutting edge of the tool in a perfect cutting action if it is placed at this angle with the bevel almost vertical.

Fig. 25. If the rest was raised, the tool handle would have to be raised to compensate and if this were taken to excess a scraping action would develop. For reasons of clarity the photographs show a larger tool than that normally used.

Stand by the lathe and give the stuff a turn by hand to make sure all is clear (a good habit to develop). Ensure all is tight – the rest and the saddle, set the lathe speed to approximately 1000 rpm and switch on. If this is the first time you have worked square stuff of this size just stand and look at it revolving for a few moments, it will make a fluttering noise as the corners pass the tool rest, and I will accept it is a bit daunting, and surely as soon as you push a tool into it, as suggested, the tool will jam and be thrown upwards. Take it from me it will not, and after a couple of minutes working you will be wondering why you ever thought woodturning was a mystique. The sharp edge will slice through those corners with an ease that will be a delight to behold.

Fig. 26. The lathe from the turner's view point. Take the tool and hold it firmly on whichever side is most natural and comfortable, (you will eventually have to be ambidexterous).

Fig. 27. My left hand, fingers round the handle, thumb on top, holds the tool in a firm grip, but not so tight as to make the knuckles whiten, and rests against my body. The tool rest hand, my right, with the index finger and thumb being the only ones used, the other three not doing anything more than just resting on the tool out of the way. Keep the index finger in contact with the tool rest under the tool with the thumb holding it, again not too tightly. By maintaining this position during the run along the stuff the tool rest hand becomes a 'fence' and guides the tool along the length of the cut at a fixed attitude ensuring the cut will be straight. If a deeper cut is required all you have to do is to lift the handle slightly.

With the tool held in this way, place it on the tool rest, just clear of the work and approximately 15cm (6in) from the end of the work; we will be working from right to left. Take your time, relax, keep your index finger in contact with the tool rest and ease the tool forward and upward through the fingers of the right hand until it you feel the cut has commenced. At this point nip the tool between the thumb and index finger and move to the left past the end of the work keeping the tool at right-angles to the work, and the tool handle in contact with your body all the way. Continue this way, stopping occasionally to admire your work and to move the tool rest in so that it is never more than 6mm ($\frac{1}{4}$in) away from the work. It is easy for me to suggest that you hold the tool gently and firmly, but I know from experience that it is only natural for folk unused to tackling a piece of square stuff to grip the tool as if someone were about to steal it; I notice my pupils knuckles go quite white with the pressure of the grip. You will find, however,

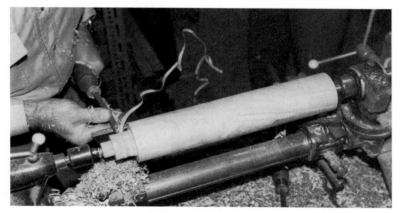

that as you progress you will be able to relax and hold the tools firmly but gently which is absolutely vital to permit freedom of movement round curves both concave and convex, and for general comfort and reduction of fatigue.

Fig. 28.   The stuff is reduced to a true cylinder so now is the time to practise taking fine cuts and to see if you can produce a finish that will require the very minimum of sanding. Notice that the shaving produced is, due to the underhand grip, passing down the middle of the tool and out of the way.

Fig. 29.   Using the overhand grip the shaving hits my little finger and curls up in front of the work making it difficult to see the tip of the tool. In practice, with a little experience, you will start to look at the top edge of the work but it does indicate the merits of the underhand grip. If you feel more confident to begin with the overhand grip use it by all means; as the confidence that comes with skill increases, you will want to use the underhand grip.
    The roughing-out gouge has many other uses other than a tool for working stuff down to a cylinder. It is also almost fool-proof and has no real vices. It is the ideal tool to practise with and to build confidence, and some projects can be completed with no other tool being required. Work away with it, try to form long convex or concave shapes – it is not too good in acute angles – but remember to keep the tool in line with the working line i.e. at 90° to the tool rest with a straight cylinder. Try varying the thickness of the shaving by simply lifting and/or lowering the handle as the cut along the work proceeds. The shaving is not important but this will give practice in the quick removal of waste. Generally just get used to cutting timber that is revolving at speed, and keep the speed for all the aforesaid at approximately 1000 rpm and, in your enthusiasm, don't forget to give the tool edge a rub from time to time.

Fig. 30.   Another use of the roughing-out gouge is that of working a small diameter up to a 90° angle of a larger diameter. The shape of the gouge makes it the ideal tool for the job in some circumstances. Not only the base of the U is used, you have sharpened all the cutting edge so you may as well use it and on a 38mm (1½in) gouge there is 63mm (2½in) of cutting edge! Plenty of practice will be required and as timber is expensive, I would suggest that for practise purposes you use any timber that is available. If when on holiday, or picnicking, you chance upon some logs; or a friend wants a tree or large bush removed leap in quick, so to speak.

Fig. 31.   Shows a large (for the purposes of demonstration) log being worked down to a true cylinder.

Fig. 32   Trued up and ready for plenty of practice.

Parting tools

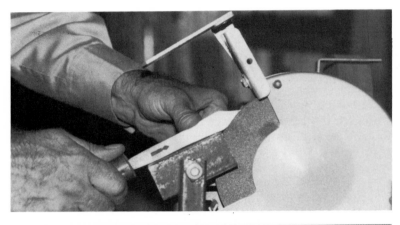

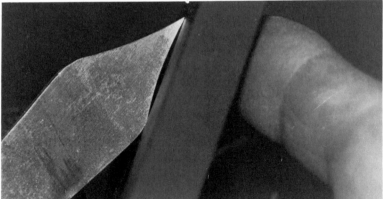

Starting with the plain parting tool of the waisted type, as this will be found to be safe and simple to use, as opposed to the parallel type that will, unless great care is taken, bind in the cut. When purchased they are not always of a shape that will be ideal and some work may be necessary to achieve the shape shown.

Fig. 33.   I will not be too specific as to the angle of grind, some folk prefer a much steeper angle than mine, experiment and see what you think. The edge must always be square with the sides and when grinding the tool is maintained in line with the direction of the wheel.

Fig. 34.   Detail showing the hollow grind. As I do not grind right up to the edge in re-establishing the hollow I only ever use a Black Arkansas to hone and, as by virtue of the waisted shape of this tool its life is limited, this method will give me at least fifty honings between grinding. I am clearly not the favourite of the toolmakers, but I hope the reader will esteem my prudence! Again, I like to hold the tool up in front of me, but if you find it more comfortable to hone as you would a bench tool, well and good.

Fig. 35.   A close-up of the parting tool in use; again, allow the finger and thumb to control the cut by a combination of lifting the tool handle and gently passing the tool through the finger and thumb as more tool is required to complete the cut.

Fig. 36. To start the parting cut hold the handle low and push the tool upwards into the work. Two cuts with the tool held on its side will prevent spelching prior to entry; then enter the tool between these cuts.

Fig. 37. As the cut progresses, feed the tool through the tool rest hand and at the same time lift the handle. In the early stages of practise leave a dowel of about 6mm ($\frac{1}{4}$in) in diameter to be finished off with the saw.

Fig. 38. After a little practise using two hands on the tool, progress to the one–handed hold using the other to hold calipers or a vernier. This will be found to be a great time-saver and is quite safe to do, the calipers will not catch and as soon as the stuff is of the right diameter just lower the handle and stop the cut, this is preferable to just taking it out of the cut by pulling back. You may find that the measured diameter of the calipers increases due to a slight vibration of the calipers rubbing until the right size is reached. This can be overcome by resting a finger on the knurled nut of the caliper which will prevent it unscrewing under vibration. Note that in Fig. 35, a long shaving is produced, but in Fig. 37 and 38 the waste is in the form of short chip shavings. This will be explored further when we come to the chisel, in the meantime don't worry about it, it is not significant.

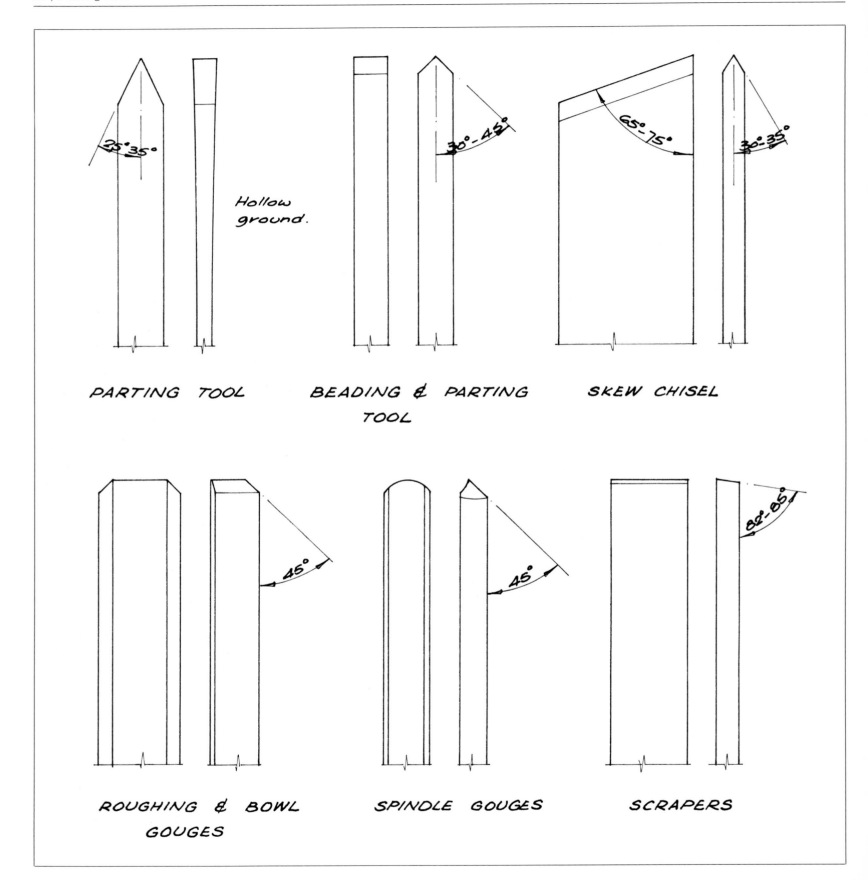

PARTING TOOL

Hollow ground.

BEADING & PARTING TOOL

SKEW CHISEL

ROUGHING & BOWL GOUGES

SPINDLE GOUGES

SCRAPERS

Beading and parting tools

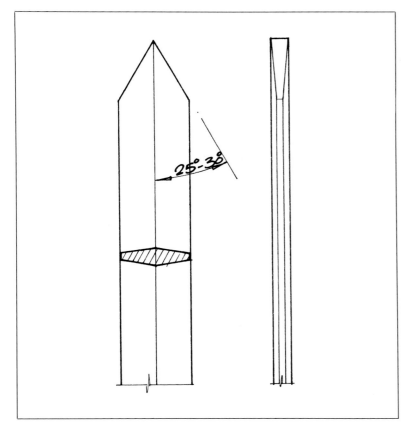

Fig. 39 (left).   Tool grinding angles.

Fig. 40 (above).   High speed steel diamond parting tool.

Why this tool is called a beading and *parting* tool I cannot imagine, it is quite the wrong shape for parting, as it is not waisted, and being 10mm ($\frac{3}{8}$in) wide the waste factor would be unacceptable if used for parting. All that being said it is the tool for working beads so let's have a look at it use for this purpose. It is ground and honed in the same way as the parting tool, and again I will not be specific as to the angle but let the reader determine his own using Fig. 39 and 40 as a guide. It is wise to mark out your practice stuff and attempt to work to the marked lines, it won't matter if you have a slip and pass them, that is what practice is for. Working beads and coves does not just give practise in working to pre-determined marks; if the work is not clearly marked out one bead will run into another, some will be larger or smaller and you will soon be in a fine old mess. Working to a precise size means the method will not vary from bead to bead in the amount of lift, roll or whatever, that needs to be applied to the tool.

Mark out a length of about a foot of practice stuff that you have previously used to perfect working square stuff down to a cylinder of about 50mm (2in) in diameter. Marking out is simple, take a pair of dividers with sharp points and set them to about 10mm ($\frac{3}{8}$in) wide; with the lathe running use them to mark even divisions along the length of the stuff, don't press too hard just clearly mark the divisions. In the middle of each division place another mark using a soft pencil. Now the length of stuff is clearly divided practise can commence. Take a thin skew chisel and working with it on the side that is most comfortable and natural, use only the point of the long corner, with the long corner down, and thrust it into all the *divider* marks to a depth of about 6mm ($\frac{1}{4}$in). Use a quick in and out movement thus avoiding heating up the thin point. Set the lathe speed to not more than 1000 rpm, slower if you have the facility, and taking the beading tool and working from right to left, rest the tool on the revolving stuff with the bevel rubbing but not cutting. The left-hand point should be just into the waste side of the *pencil* mark. Your starting position is now established, i.e. the angle that you will need to present the tool to the work. The tool rest height is up to you, but I would suggest starting about

20mm (¾in) below the top of the work; after practice you may find it convenient or comfortable to raise or lower it to accommodate your own particular style.

Fig. 41.   Shows the tool in just such a position.

Fig. 42.   The cut has started, the handle is being lifted and the tool is being rolled to the left and at the same time pushed very gently in the direction of the cut. When working in this direction the handle is held about three or four degrees to the right, see Fig. 47.

Fig. 43.   The completion of the left-hand side of the bead, the tool is completely on its side, the handle is horizontal and the point of the tool is in the base of the left-hand side of the bead.

Fig. 44.   Detail showing the marking of the bead divisions, and the cuts produced by the long corner of the skew chisel; the cutting of the bead is just starting, note the handle of the tool is held a little to the right, (from the turner's side) this will point the tool *out* of the bead very slightly. Only the point of the tool is ever used, never the cutting edge as this is bound to cause a snag.

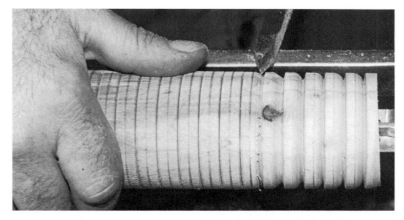

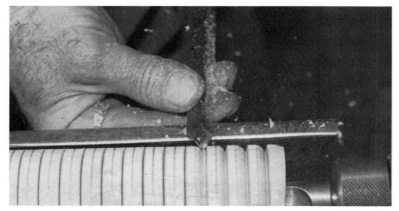

Fig. 45.   Half way round, the tool is rolled and the handle raised in a continuous movement, with a little pressure from the thumb in the direction of the cutting.

Fig. 46.   Almost at the base of the bead; it is at this point that a snag is most likely to happen which will spoil the work beyond repair.

Fig. 47.   If the cutting part of the tool is allowed to contact and/or the tool is allowed to point *into* the bead it will follow its natural course uphill, it cannot go anywhere else. When this happens, stop the lathe at once, study the snag and, turning the work by hand let the tool 'fit' into the error. The illustration shows how the tool fits perfectly into the snag. Note, too, that the tool is pointed *into* the bead so the error was inevitable. Whenever an error occurs, stop the lathe and using this technique try to figure out why. It is easy for me to talk as I know how vexing snags can be, but a calm investigation of the problem will be better than stamping on your hat!

I have not detailed the other half of the bead because I have found that it is by far the best to practise on one side only to start with, the other side is exactly the same procedure but going in a completely different direction. Until you have mastered one direction to try and reverse in the opposite direction is asking for confusion and frustration none of which will do anything to help you to improve your skill. Far better to stick to just working one side, and perfect it; you will then be full of confidence and well practised and will be able to achieve the other side of the bead with ease. At the risk of repeating myself, take your time and relax; it is doubtful that you will get it right in the first few minutes, leave a bead that has gone wrong and go on to the next, and, above all, enjoy your learning. There is a lot of satisfaction in being able to do it, but there is a lot of fun to be had just learning, and the satisfaction of having mastered any skill or technique, is to be savoured.

Fig. 48.   The tool in use as a parting tool. This is the way you would use it to prepare a length of stuff to mount it in the split rings of the 6-in-1 patent chuck which requires a groove 45mm ($1\frac{3}{4}$in) diameter, 10mm ($\frac{3}{8}$in) in from the end of the stuff and 10mm ($\frac{3}{8}$in) wide. This tool is ideal for the purpose.

The spindle gouge

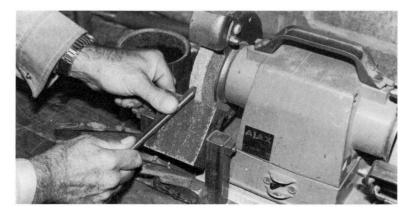

Let us start straight away with the grinding, we can discuss the applications of the tool as we proceed. The angle of bevel will vary slightly for the different purposes that this tool will be used but start with about 45°, the same as the roughing-out gouge, for general use. Whilst the rest is used and this will maintain a positive angle the shape of the ground area will be to a large extent dependent on the angle that the tool is applied to the wheel, and on the dexterity of the operator.

Fig. 49.   For a fingernail shape apply the gouge to the wheel canted slightly to the right and presented at an angle of approximately 25°–30°.

Fig. 50.   Work the tool round the wheel so that it is completely on its back when the centre is reached and the tool is in line with the wheel.

Fig. 51.   Continue to roll the tool past this point and to swing the handle to the finish position. Not an easy technique but when mastered it will render a perfectly hollow grind and a fine shape to the business end of the tool. To save costly tool steel practise using a 12mm ($\frac{1}{2}$in) bolt. Try to acquire the technique without cheating; keep the bolt cool, do not apply heavy pressure, and treat it as if it were one of your finest tools and, of course, only grind up to the centre of the bolt's diameter as this will mirror the actual tool. This practice piece can also be used to experiment with in producing different, or more severe shapes. The angle will, of course, be governed by the rest, but it is clear that the greater or smaller the angle it is applied to the wheel will produce variation of shape to a considerable degree. Hone in the same way as previously discussed and when regrinding becomes necessary, do so in the same way but, of course, not right up to the edge.

Fig. 52.   The spindle gouge is used on its side (slightly exaggerated in photograph) to effect a guillotine action of cut. This will render a very smooth work surface and prolong the life of the cutting edge. The lathe speed for all the following is 1500 rpm, and I am using a revolving centre.

Fig. 53.   In close-up and again in considerable exaggeration to illustrate the guillotine effect which will sometimes be found necessary to produce a fine smooth finish on a length of stuff with interlocking grain or a knot or two. It should be used with caution as it confines the cutting edge to a very small area and ribbing is likely, to avoid this the tool should be traversed very slowly.

Fig. 54.   Side view close-up, and at about the right angle of presentation for average working. It is interesting to note that while a distinct and clean shaving is coming off there is also some dust from this particular timber due, possibly, to its being a little over dry.

Fig. 55.   Working the smoothing cut in the opposite direction, but with the same hand at the tool rest, and with the tool presented at about the correct angle. Note how a sharp tool will cut cleanly through a knot surrounded by undulating grain.

Fig. 56.   Working a cove. The start must be made with the tool completely on its side, and the tool rest positioned to permit the *centre* of the crescent shape of the gouge, or the tip if you like, to enter. If either of these points are missed the tool will, in all probability, skid to one side. It will also be found helpful if the gouge is first entered into the work at an angle so that when working the right-hand side as here, keep the handle to the right, and work a slot.

Fig. 57.   This is one of those cuts that necessitate using the tool on both sides of the body, so I hope you have been practising. Change hands and repeat as in Fig. 56. The angle of presentation is again somewhat exaggerated for clarity. Timbers will vary, some will be found very workable and with few vices, others will be 'sneaky' and try to catch you out, you will get to know them in time, this is what working in wood is all about, every piece is a new experience.

Fig. 58.   Return to the right-hand side, replace the tool in the slot, starting with the tool handle slightly to the right and with a scooping action bring it to an angle of 90° to the rest. As the cut proceeds, roll it in a quarter arc lowering the handle as the centre is reached to stop the cut. Do not try to cut uphill, timber doesn't like it.

Fig. 59..   The other side is completed in like manner, working to the base of the cove only. You will possibly find that at first you will be chasing a small upstand at the base of the cove, or a second run down will be required. This is quite normal, indeed with large section coves, or beads for that matter, it will be necessary to enlarge or make several passes over the work to complete. Don't try too hard, take your time, follow the cut with the eye as it progresses, and think of the tool as an extension of a finger and use it for working coves as you would scoop jam out of the pot, but don't get caught doing it!

The following cut is well worth perfecting as it has a multitude of uses and will save hours of sanding on any project where this part will be exposed to view, in the tops of pepper mills, boxes, etc.

Fig. 60. To effect a clean cut across the work the spindle gouge has its advantages over the chisel, it is almost impossible to snag it. It may be a help to cut a light slot with a parting tool presented on its side, or with a skew chisel, long corner down, this will give the gouge a starting point and prevent any skidding sideways. Only take light cuts for the smoothest surface.

Fig. 61. Again the tool must be completely on its side and entered into the prepared slot, then with the bevel of the tool in line with the end of the work, the handle at approximately 45° to the rest and the rest set to permit the tool to enter approximately 6mm (¼in) above the centre line

of the work, push it gently across the end grain. This cut will produce a finish on the work that will require only the minimum of abrasive to complete the work and for a really hard wood 0000 gauge steel wool will be all that is necessary. The tool handle is maintained in the horizontal throughout.

Fig. 62. If the end of the work needs to be rounded over the work can be approached in like manner. Start with the handle low, about 15°, and not quite on its side. Lift the handle slightly to commence the cut, at the same time keeping it very slightly to the left, which will prevent the tool pointing into the work resulting in a snag.

Fig. 63. Try to keep the cut on the lower, or right-hand side of the tool, and progressively roll the gouge, following the line of working with the bevel which will be the guide, it wants to be just off the full rubbing position.

Fig. 64. The cut almost at completion. You may be wondering how a shaving is produced from end grain. A study of this picture will show that while we are working round an area of end grain, the cut is occuring from side grain, as the cut is under the tool and not to the side of it. Similarly in Fig. 53 and 54, the bevel of the tool is doing the guiding but the cut is being made underneath which could be seen if the photo was taken from the level of the tool rest.

Fig. 65. As the cut progresses the handle must be lifted to bring the point or centre of the tool along the centre line of the work. For the finishing cut only the lightest of cuts is required and this will produce the really superfine finish that we want.

Fig. 66. The gouge can be taken right through to finish as in Fig. 120 leaving no visible holding mark to mar the work. Alternatively with a skew chisel as here, with long corner down and using the bevel of the tool as a guide, the small pip that remains can be reduced to a minimum with a clean cut. The remainder can finally be removed on the bench with a sharp bench chisel, do not try to break it off as this will pull the grain out and leave a mark. In practice, however, such methods are seldom necessary as with a pepper mill, for instance, there would be a hole for the drive mechanism in the end of the work, in which the centre would be running. All that you would have to beware of would be hitting the centre as the finishing cut was effected. In the case of boxes or knobs the work would be held in one or other of the patent chucks that are available, or in a home-made mandrel or jig, thus the entire end would be exposed, unsupported by the tailstock, and it is a simple matter to work all round, finish and polish before taking the work off the lathe. We will, of course, have a close look at all this later in the book.

The chisel

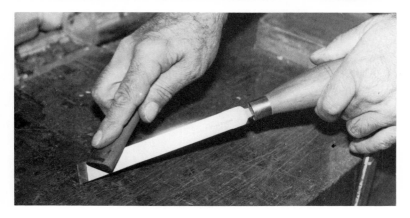

Preparation of the chisel

Fig. 67.   Re-set the grinder rest to the required angle, if necessary using the tool to be ground as a template, or any other chisel that is prepared to the same angle. If the tool is skew-shaped, maintain the shape by retaining the angle square with the face of the wheel as shown. As with the other tools place one finger behind the platform, or in a position that will enable pressure from the thumb to exert a pinch action. Ensure that your finger is *clear of the wheel*. The other hand is kept up close to the platform, and the index finger is used as a fence to render complete control and pressure.

Fig. 68.   Seen from the side. It will be obvious that this is an accurate method, the only part of the grinding operation that must be left to judgement is that the ground area on both sides of the tool must meet in the centre to give a perfectly balanced tool edge. Again, it will not be necessary to grind right up to the edge, just re-establish the hollow and then hone in the same way as discussed earlier, using a flat fine stone. Take care to bridge the stone across the hollow grind.

Fig. 69.   With new chisels it is wise to remove the arris, the sharp edges of the tool; this will allow a smooth passage along the tool rest and is especially important with the new HSS tools available, as these are hard enough to bite into the softer steel of the average tool rest. For skew chisels it will only be necessary to perform this operation on the edge adjacent to the short corner, as shown; for square chisels, which will be used either way up and in both directions, all four edges should be softly rounded.

Using the chisel

The turner's chisel is in effect his smoothing plane. It will be used in two shapes, either ground skewed or straight across, both have their merits. Taking the skew first, this shape has the disadvantage that for normal chisel work only two-thirds of the ground and honed edge will be used. For other work, however, the long corner will have several uses as will be seen.

The straight across is the shape for smoothing work between centres, all that has to be remembered is to present it to the work in a skewed mode. It has the distinct advantage that the whole edge can be used, in either direction or either way up, whichever way you care to look at it.

I am often asked what the correct speed is to work a given diameter. To say that it is impossible to answer is not being very helpful, nevertheless it poses a problem to the beginner, and so far I have indicated a speed in each of the sections we have covered. I hope by now the reader will have appreciated that high speeds are not the panacea for all ills, in fact quite the reverse. The following photographs show the result of working the same piece of stuff, with the same tool (honed between speeds) at five different speeds.

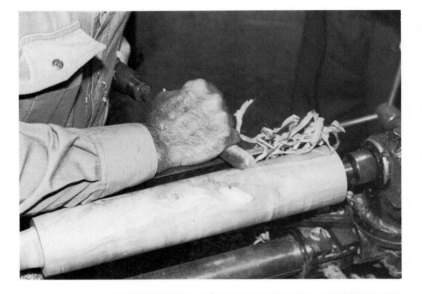

Fig. 70.   Speed 350 rpm, cutting quite nicely, tool staying cool and not losing its edge too quickly. The finish is not good, and due to the low speed the stuff is starting to oval and the tool is not easy to control. This is a nice practice speed but should ideally be used on a larger diameter.

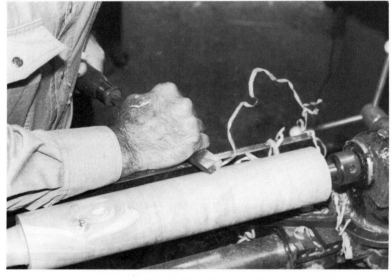

Fig. 71.   Speed 650 rpm, fast enough to bring the stuff to a true cylinder again; the shaving is long and unbroken, tool cool with no noticeable loss of cutting edge. The finish is good but not as I would like it, and some sanding would be necessary.

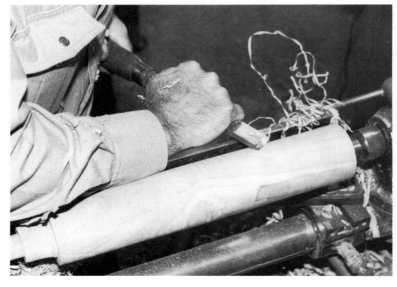

Fig. 72.   Speed 1000 rpm, similar to Fig. 71 and comfortable to work leaving a finish behind the tool that requires the very minimum of sanding. Note the fine, unbroken shaving, clearly the optimum speed for this timber.

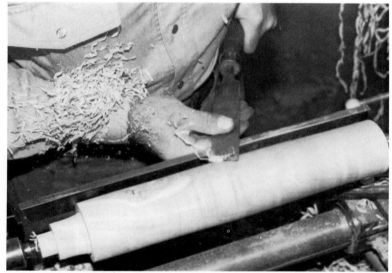

Fig. 73.   Speed 1600 rpm, tool quickly became warm with the result that the cutting edge suffered and it was not nearly as easy to control. The shaving is broken and some dust has formed. The surface is as good as at 1000 rpm, but no better, and there is a slight tendency to chip the knots.

Fig. 74.   Speed 2500 rpm, again no real improvement to the finished surface, the tool heats quickly, but is not so difficult to control. It slices cleanly through the grain around the knots but, again, chipped the knots.

Fig. 75.   A different timber of the same dimensions worked at the optimum speed of 1000 rpm shown in Fig. 72. Note no shavings, but an excellent finish from the tool.

I should mention that for the purpose of the experiment and to throw a shaving upward for clarity, I had to grind a shorter bevel on the tool than I would normally have, this meant an overhand grip was necessary to hold the tool down in all but one of the photographs. The perfect speed for this diameter, approximately 63mm (2½in) on both timbers was 1000 rpm, but I would emphasis that this is not necessarily the rule. Do not assume that 1000 rpm is the ideal speed for this diameter on *all* timbers, but it is a good speed to start with if in doubt, or you are having problems with a particular piece of stuff. I hope it will also indicate that long fine shavings will not always be produced, nor is it an indication that you are getting things right if you do produce shavings. The important thing is the finish from the tool, shavings or no shavings; if this is right, that is all you need be concerned with and not all timbers will produce shavings. Far more important is an appreciation of peripheral speed. For between-centres work this is less important than it is for bowl work as long as it is realised that the circumference is travelling at a greater speed than the centre. We look at this in greater detail in bowl turning on page 52. In the meantime unless the work between centres is of very large proportions, or the shape is such that the tool will be working from large diameter to small, as in the chapter on table lamps, don't worry about it.

Fig. 76. Set the speed to 1000 rpm or a little less, for working on stuff of about 60mm (2½in) diameter with a 38mm (1½in) skew chisel. Holding the chisel, thumb on top and fingers against the tool rest, rest the tool on the revolving stuff in a bevel-rubbing but not cutting mode. This will enable you to feel the contact with the work. Bring the weight of the thumb down on the tool and thus on to the tool rest. With the lightest pressure on the work and keeping the weight on the tool rest, gently draw the tool back towards you and at the same time lift the handle very slightly to maintain contact with the work. Note the position of the tape under my thumb in relation to the tool rest, it is about dead centre at the start of drawing back.

Fig. 77. Continue to draw back while lifting the tool and it will be felt that the shape of the bevel 'fits' the work, and will feel right in the hands. The amount of draw back from the rubbing position to the cutting position is minimal; note the position of the tape, it has only moved a fraction backwards, and the cut has commenced.

Fig. 78. Draw back slightly more and the cut is producing a full shaving, or if using a timber that does not throw a shaving you will feel and see a clean finish behind the passage of the tool. The width of the tool rest is about 10mm (⅜in) and if you look at the difference between the position of the tape in Fig. 76 to the cutting position in Fig. 78 it has barely travelled 3mm (⅛in).

Fig. 79. The same sequence seen from the side. Little more than the bevel is rubbing to position the tool and permit you to relax and take your time when drawing the tool backwards, very slowly and under complete control. The left-hand index finger is acting as a fence, and the amount of draw back and consequent lifting of the tool will determine the depth of cut, which for this tool in normal use will not need to be excessive.

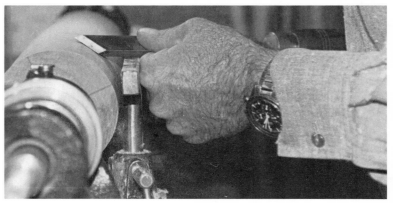

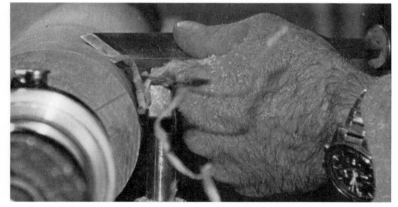

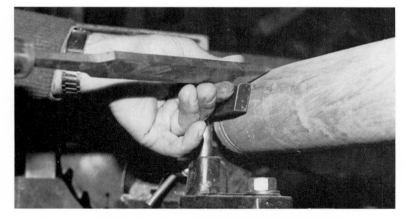

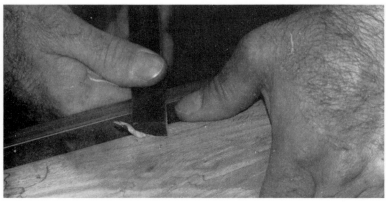

Fig. 80. As the cut commences draw the tool along the work, in this case from right to left. Keep the tool handle against the body, the right hand with thumb on top positioned just behind the ferrule and exerting gentle pressure downwards.

Fig. 81. Providing you do not alter the lift of the handle or the position of the forefinger and thumb of the left hand, the cut will be of uniform thickness throughout, and the tool should be taken right off the end of the work.

Fig. 82. The position as seen from below. Only the leading edge of the tool contacts the tool rest and only part of the chisel from the short corner to a little more than half-way across its width can be used. Try to avoid any pressure on the work, keep the weight on the tool and on the tool rest, and as you traverse the work the tool rest will control the cut to a great extent leaving you free to guide the tool.

Fig. 83. If you can persuade a friend to turn the lathe by hand, or as here turn it yourself, use the tool as described to try a few experiments yourself. A lot can be learned this way, and working in slow motion will enable you to understand the mechanics of what we have been discussing. It is also a good time to study how a snag with the chisel can occur. Continue to turn the stuff but allow the cut to go across the half-way mark, you will find the tool will take control, let it, and the cut will progress up the cutting edge to the long corner, when it will grab and bury itself in the stuff leaving a nasty mark. That is all it will do, it won't hurt you, other than a little pride perhaps and it happens to me with monotonous regularity when I am not paying attention! It is vexing, and can, of course, spoil a job if it happens near the finishing, but now you know how *not* to let it happen.

  Smoothing cuts are by no means the only work for the chisel, so as we are now at the end of the preliminary preparation of our tools, and with a bit of practise behind us, before we go on to actually make something, let's put a few exercises together in one length of stuff, without working to a high degree of accuracy so that if the inevitable mistake occurs, it will not cause disappointment.

Fig. 84.   A finished pommel, such would be used for stool or chair legs, etc.

Fig. 85.   Take a piece of stuff about 50mm (2in) square, and for the best results ensure that it is square all round. Carefully cross mark both ends and set up between centres. Select a speed of between 1000 and 1500 rpm and take a skew chisel, long corner down, and push it into the stuff with the tool at right-angles to the work. The cleft produced will be of no great depth due to the wedge shape of the tool. Enlarge the cleft by taking light cuts from both sides, this is shown in Fig. 96 and 97, until the cut is almost deep enough to mark all round the stuff, but not quite deep enough to complete. This profile occasions working into a right-angle and stopping before the other side of the work is marked, so a little waste left will not go amiss.

Fig. 86.   Change to a roughing-out gouge and with it used well on its side work carefully almost up to the cleft. (With very large diameter stuff, such as would be used for a table leg, this is the best way to reduce the waste and is preferable to enlarging the cleft with the chisel.) Work deeper than the mark made by the cleft but do not work right up into the right-angle corner, leaving about 2mm ($\frac{1}{16}$in) of waste and reduce the stuff to within a fraction of a true cylinder.

Fig. 87.   Take a newly-sharpened skew, and with the handle to the left take a fine finishing cut or two. Sanding this part is not at all easy and will have the effect of rounding over the sharp profiles; thus the better the finish from the tool the better the job. Then, as in Fig. 94 and Fig. 106, use the short corner of the skew and, keeping the tool as square with the work as possible so that it will form its own stop, make light cuts to complete at the junction of the two cuts. It may be found that you will be chasing the mark left by the previous cut, i.e. when smoothing the cylinder the short corner of the skew will mark the shoulder of the pommel, this will be removed with a cut round the pommel only, to mark the cylinder. This can be further complicated as by using the short corner a lot of shavings will build up in front of the tool making it difficult to see what you are doing. It is not the easiest of cuts to make but by taking your time and making light cuts, you will master it in the end, and you will then experience the pleasure that comes with a new skill acquired.

Fig. 88.   I prefer the skew chisel for the making of beads and I always use the long corner but some craftsmen like to use the short corner, I suppose it is what you get used to. Try it both ways and see what suits you best. The size of the bead is marked out and with a pencil line in the centre which must be left in, for this exercise anyway. Make the two cuts as described on page 21. With the tool angled *away* from the direction of working, lay it on the work in a bevel-rubbing mode, and using the point only of the long corner throughout, position this just into the waste side of the pencil mark. Lift the handle of the tool slowly and as the cut commences continue to lift, at the same time revolve to the right and push gently to the right.

Fig. 89.   Half-way round, the lift of the handle is hardly noticeable.

Fig. 90.   Finish off the bead with the skew upright. The advantage of using only the long corner is that all through the cut the tool presentation angle is pointed out of the direction of working, and due to the shape of the skewed end of the tool the angle of this shape is also pointed out of the work, i.e. it slopes backwards and should be almost impossible for the tool to snag. If the two preliminary cuts require cleaning up or to make the bead deeper or larger, the method given in Fig. 95 and 96 can be used.

Fig. 91.   Next to the bead a cove should be worked. I have marked out the work and while this is not absolutely necessary it will help your confidence to do so and give you some experience in working to limits as would be required if, for instance, making four legs all matching.

Fig. 92. Reduce a little more of the stuff to a rough cylinder, not all of it as some of the square end remaining will be required later. This reduces the possibility of getting a rap on the knuckles from it while you are working which can be very painful and the sooner you do it and get it over with, the sooner you will make sure it does not happen again. Now for a quadrant to join up with the cylinder. It is more or less the same technique as working one half of a bead but as it has to join the cylinder with no visible marking at the junction, we will have to use the short corner of the tool. If you ever have to do this cut either at the pommel end or as we are doing now, and you are working with an awkward timber that is making the job tiresome, a way round it is to change the design slightly to incorporate a V-cut at the junction, see Fig. 95. With the tool angled away from the work, and taking a light cut, roll it round the quadrant shape making it deeper with each cut, and not marking the cylinder.

Fig. 93. The cut in close-up.

Fig. 94. Work up to the quadrant profile with the skew presented as much at right-angles to the line of working as possible, smoothing the cylinder at the same time.

Fig. 95. A small V-cut can be made at the junction, and this can also apply to the junction of the pommel and cylinder both for decorative and other reasons, sometimes there is a lot of sense in the saying 'the end justifies the means'. An alternative would be to work a bead to coincide at this junction. Whichever method is used it should not be considered a substitute for the right way. The small bead is worked, but not coinciding with the junction of the quadrant and cylinder. It is good practice to work beads in a confined space as shown as if care is not taken you will mark the face of the quadrant while doing so.

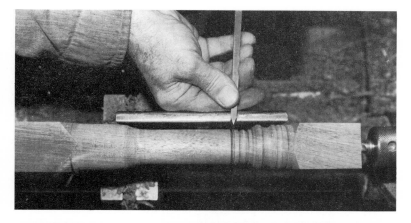

Fig. 96.   For the V-cut we must again present the skew long corner down and dead square to the work. Once a cut is made it can be further enlarged by taking thin cuts from either side alternately, going in a little deeper each time. Light cuts are necessary as this will render a clean smooth side to the V and minimise sanding thus leaving a sharp profile to the finished work.

Fig. 97.   Close-up of the V-cut shows that the thinner the section of the chisel the better. I buy the thinnest tool that I can get for skews. The square or straight across chisels do not matter so much as I use them mainly for smoothing work.

Fig. 98.   The top of the two front chair legs will be exposed and therefore a clean surface must be produced. Take a very sharp skew, and with the long corner down and the handle held to the left, take a light cut to start with. In the photograph the first cut can be seen hanging on the tailstock, this is the second cut which is now in to the full depth of the overall size of the stuff. The handle can now be brought to a position square with the work; there will be no fear of the tool skidding to the left as it has the solid timber to support it.

Fig. 99.   Continue to make as many cuts as are necessary, either to work to a marked line on the stuff or to be able to fell the work off with a final cut right through leaving the surface clean for final sanding by hand.

Fig. 100.   For further decoration and practise at leaving a sharp profile with no broken edges, a section can be worked to a cylinder. With the skew, long corner down, just nip the four corners of the square stuff. As this cut need only be made with the lightest pressure the skew can be presented with the handle slightly to the right. This will allow the shape of the tool to commence the cut with most of the V effect into the waste. Then with the beading tool, square to the work and handle low, take a couple of light cuts. If the timber used is a little soft or shreddy it may be necessary to use the point of the skew again to cut further into the end grain, but with most hardwoods this shouldn't be needed.

Fig. 101.   The finished cut in close-up, mostly worked with the parting tool. Any slight spelch will be removed when the flat section of the work is sanded. Take care when sanding the cylinder not to allow the paper to mark the end grain or to damage the sharp corners of the square – and watch your knuckles!

As this is a practice piece, work the end down to a cylinder with the roughing-out gouge. We can now discuss working tapers, but just to make it interesting we will again work into a corner.

Fig. 102.   Take a thin parting tool and work a parting cut, you might like to do this to a specific depth holding calipers in one hand.

Fig. 103.   The taper can be worked with a roughing-out gouge particularly if the stuff is giving trouble. However, try it with the skew chisel, resting it on the work in a bevel-rubbing mode to position it before commencing the cut. As you work to the left, continually lift the handle as the cut proceeds, this will send the tool deeper into the work.

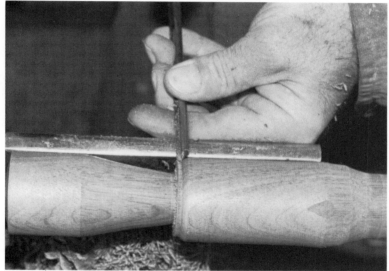

There is a limit to the amount of lift that can be exerted, so don't go at it like a bull at a gate. Continue in this way taking care to keep the tool under control, and do not let the short corner strike the end grain of the junction.

Fig. 104. This time we can use a gouge to work the quadrant and complete this cut almost to the base of the junction, taking care, of course, not to mark the cylinder.

Fig. 105. The cut in close-up. You may find that it is possible to effect the cut completely with the gouge, but due to its rounded shape it is not easy to see what is happening. Try it and see how you get on, remember that only the tip of the gouge must end up at the junction between the end grain and the tapered cylinder.

Fig. 106. A final cleaning up with the skew chisel, short corner down, allowing the bevel to guide the tool round the shape of the quadrant.

These are not the simplest set of exercises, but when perfected and used, either singly or in combination, they will be the basis of many design configurations. They are not easy but with a bit of practise, you will be wondering why you ever thought them unattainable, and anyway if you were not determined to master the craft you would not have read thus far, would you?

Keep cool, stop when things go wrong and ponder the problem, remember you are not alone, we all make mistakes so try to learn by them. Some timbers work better than others, and even two pieces from the same log can vary considerably. Don't try to run before you can walk, and don't let anyone rush you, take your time and enjoy to the full learning a new cut or technique; when you can do it with ease some of that enjoyment will be lost forever. It will also be obvious that in practising this exercise you will now have perfected all the cuts that will be required in the making of a table or chair leg, etc. It is now only a matter of putting them into some design form.

Scrapers

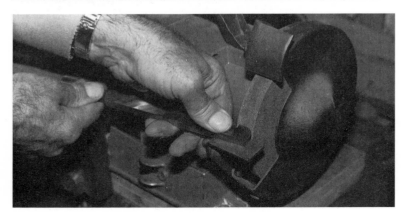

Fig. 107.   Scrapers must be prepared with the same care as all tools. That being said, experience has shown me that these tools can be used straight from the grinder with no further preparation. The back, or top of the tool, the part that is taking the edge, must be perfectly *flat*, but as we will be using it without honing it does not, thankfully, have to be polished. Prior to grinding always remove the old worn-out burr on a fine stone and take care to wipe off any oil before presenting the tool to the wheel as this will quickly clog it. The fine wheel recommended in Fig. 1 should be used.

Fig. 108.   I find the rest supplied with the grinder is big and stable enough for this work. Place your finger under the table adjusting nut, *not* under the table as this would quickly result in a very short finger!

Fig. 109.   The tool is placed in the start position, finger and thumb of the left hand keep the tool tight and level on the table. This is a half-round high speed steel inserted tool.

Fig. 110. The right hand is used to swing the tool through the arc required for this shape. Only light pressure is required and as many passes as are deemed necessary can be made, quenching between passes.

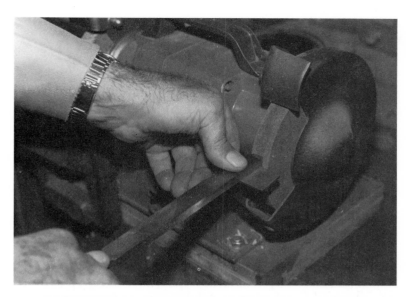

Fig. 111. This method will produce a grind of only one angle and each pass will turn up a progressively finer burr which is, in effect, the cutting edge. Once the angle is established, two or three passes will provide an edge that will hollow out an egg cup on one grinding only, perhaps with a final cut from a newly-sharpened tool.

Scrapers

It is frequently said that scraping timber to shape should be avoided at all costs. Such a practice will not give a good finish on the work, it is crude and dangerous, and very un-professional That being said, there are situations where a scraper must be used and this creates what I know to be a dilemma among aspiring turners.

Fig. 112. It is, of course, not possible to cover all the situations where scrapers will or will not be required, but let us consider some situations where they can be used. Sometimes, due to the design form, or for no other reason than being a bit afraid of tackling a particular profile with a cutting tool if it is a difficult area to get at or there is a knot in the most awkward place, a scraper could be used. It must *always* be presented to the work in a negative rake, handle higher than the cutting edge. The angle will be a matter of experience with different timbers but scrapers must *never* be presented with the handle lower than the cutting edge. This photograph shows that a fine cut producing shavings can be produced on some timbers and, as we are here working a cove very near to the edge of the work, if you are not too confident with a gouge, a scraper will suffice. The finished work will not be as fine as if a cutting tool were used, but it certainly will not be a disaster.

The following photographs show situations where it is sometimes considered possible to use the scraper. In most cases the work is better carried out with another tool and, as will be seen, combined with another accessory.

There are many articles that you will want to make that will involve working on the unsupported end of the work, such as goblets, boxes, etc. For this purpose some form of chuck will be required, and there are several available; here I am using the 6-in-1, available from Craft Supplies. The workpiece is prepared to be mounted in this chuck; this, of course, is but one of the six functions. The stuff is mounted between centres and worked to a cylinder, and the headstock end squared to within a little of the drive centre. End grain must be square with the face of the body of the chuck.

Fig. 113.   From the headstock end measure 10mm ($\frac{3}{8}$in) in. A beading tool is just the right width for the 10mm ($\frac{3}{8}$in) wide rebate required and as the cut we are working is not too deep, it will not bind in the cut, see Fig. 48. Set the calipers or vernier to a diameter of 45mm ($1\frac{3}{4}$) and with a skew, long corner down, produce a nick on the measured lines. With the tool held handle low to let the bevel rub, position the tool and, using both hands, lift the handle to commence the cut. When into the work by 6mm ($\frac{1}{4}$in) remove the tool. Take the vernier in one hand, replace the tool in the slot formed in the same way as before, lift the handle and when the vernier slips over the working diameter, just lower the tool handle and remove it from the cut.

Fig. 114.   Other sizes of split rings are available, for this exercise I am using the 45mm ($1\frac{3}{4}$in) diameter.

Fig. 115.   Test for fit, the rings must close completely with a snug fit to the worked rebate, no force is necessary, or desirable. You could work this rebate with a scraper, particularly as we are not looking for a fine finish, but it simply isn't necessary. Scrapers *must* be held with two hands so it would mean that you would have to keep putting the tool down to pick up the vernier. There is also a fear that for this sort of cut that requires a flat base a square scraper would have to be used, and if it were to bind in the cut it could be most unpleasant, and to some extent dangerous, thus I would not recommend a scraper for this purpose.

Fig. 116.   The object of the split rings is not to grip the work by compressing the rings together. When fitted to the work as suggested the tightening of the clamping ring, which has a matching dovetail section, pulls the work back into the chuck body clamping it to the face indicated.

Fig. 117.   The clamping ring is in position and the split rings in the prepared slot. If, for any reason, the work was of larger diameter preventing the clamping ring to be fitted as shown it will, of course, be necessary to work approximately 35mm (1⅜in) of the stuff from the headstock end to a diameter of 63mm (2½in).

Fig. 118.   I find it is good practice to assemble the work hand tight in the chuck, then bring up the tailstock to give a light push and to perfectly align, then tighten the chuck with the C spanners provided, again excessive force is quite unnecessary.

Fig. 119.   The tailstock can now be withdrawn and the end of the work finished, either with a chisel, preferably a skew chisel long corner down, presented to the work in a bevel-rubbing mode for complete control, and then by moving the handle to the right a fine cut can be taken and a polished surface will result. This is certainly not a job for a scraper as with the end of the work unsupported, and of this length, it is most unwise to try.

Fig. 120.   Alternatively the spindle gouge can be used as we have seen in Fig. 60 and 61. Note the gossamer-fine shaving produced from the very light pressure applied to the 10mm (⅜in) gouge. These two earlier photographs will indicate that again a scraper is unnecessary.

Fig. 121. With the round-nosed scraper, and again indicating that a fine shaving will be produced, therefore a reasonable finish, work round the end grain. I would not recommend a straight scraper for this work as it will be obvious that there is a limit as to how far it is possible to work with the tailstock supporting, which it must be if using a scraper unless you have some experience. Only the side of the tool is used, note the uniformity of the shaving indicating a very sharp tool and a controlled pressure.

Fig. 122. In close-up the fine edge, almost knife-like that we have been aiming at is very slightly chipped, and I took great care to try to produce as clean a finish as possible. While in the photograph the two areas look similar, the finish from the two cutting tools used was much superior.

Fig. 123. Part off some of the length and reduce this piece of stuff to a dimension that is more convenient to work with the end unsupported. A parting tool is used and in no circumstances should a scraper be used for this cut. Keep the handle low to start, support it against the body for complete control when working with one hand. With the tailstock withdrawn place one hand under just clearing the revolving timber, and, using the parting tool, the tailstock end will gentle fall into your hand.

Fig. 124. Let us assume we wish to hollow out an egg-cup, say, and wish to use a scraper for the purpose. The round-nosed is best to start the hollowing. The grip is much the same as I advocate with all tools, tool rest hand nipping and becoming the fence, handle hand supporting and guiding. The use of all turning tools wants to be gentle and none more so than the scraper. Use lots of light cuts, thick heavy ones will end in misery.

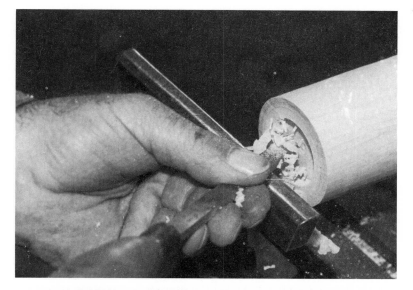

Fig. 125.   If the hollowing needs to be straight sided a tool ground straight across or perhaps better, as shown here upside down, a skewed end tool will be required. If the diameter is small and as scrapers will of necessity be at least 5mm ($\frac{3}{16}$ in) thick, it will be necessary to grind away the underside to an angle that will allow the point to contact the working line.

Fig. 126.   With some of the waste removed with the round-nosed tool, use the point or long corner only of the skew-nose, to gently push into the work. If necessary when in about 3mm ($\frac{1}{8}$ in) carefully swing the handle to the right to bring the whole cutting edge to bear.

Fig. 127.   The tool rest fingers stay in the same place, the tool is pushed through them and they are used as the pivot for the tool.

Fig. 128.   A flat-bottomed housing completed and, I would suggest, a most difficult section to work with any other tool. For clarity the recess is shallow, but by continuing the process it could be deeper, and I would further suggest that the deeper you go, the more 'impossible' this section would become to work with any tool other than a scraper. To sum up then, scrapers are an integral part of the turner's tool kit, properly prepared and presented to the work, where the need arises, they will give good service. They should never be considered amateur's tools, and should never be used where a cutting tool can be used to advantage. Further use of scrapers will be discussed when we come to bowl work.

Bowls

Bowl turning is, perhaps, the most contentious area of woodturning. Much has been written on the subject, and the recent introduction of the new HSS (high speed steel) bowl gouges has been confusing for some beginners. I am not really sure that I have all the answers, any more than I am in any way convinced that there is a standard method or, indeed, that the so-called, long and strong deep-fluted bowl gouge, is the only tool with which bowls can be produced. This, then is an account of *my* approach to the work, and in an effort to get as much as possible into the space available, I will start with a blank that is not in the conventional form of the usual bowl blank mounted for working. This will serve to indicate two ideas for the reader to consider, but I must emphasise that for the complete beginner, starting with a small, 150mm (6in) diameter blank, no more than 50mm (2in) thick, and mounted in the lathe in a true disc form, will be the best and safest way to start.

Bowl turning is fun and requires both skill and imagination, but due to the size of the material used it is also expensive. The first thing to consider is availability of material. Not everyone lives near a timber yard or sawmill, however, when on holiday or out in the car keep a lookout for such places as a visit will pay dividends and a reasonably-priced stock of timber can be accumulated. Don't overlook the firewood pile when visiting sawyers. The first cut off the log is known as a slab and will be found in various sizes and thicknesses, and while it is not in the conventional form it will be found to be ideal and this is what I will be using for this chapter. Due to the natural state of the material perfect configuration of grain formation will often result, and as this formation is of little use to the sawyer to convert into plank they can be obtained almost free of charge. I seldom make bowls from anything else.

Fig. 129.   The blank when dry will have moved to some extent and a flat surface must be worked for the initial mounting. With the stuff in the vice, plane this area so that at least the centre part is true. I use a wooden jack plane for this purpose fitted with a crescent-shaped iron that will

take a thick cut, thus reducing the material quickly, finishing, if necessary, with a smoothing plane with a straight iron. As it is a flat and not a finished surface we want, planing *across* the grain will be found best on most timbers, especially those that are hard or with interlocking grain.

Fig. 130.   With a straightedge or the plane held on its side, check the centre area is flat.

Fig. 131.   Cross mark, and using a compass, scribe a true disc and cut it out with either a bandsaw, if you have one, or a bowsaw. I have not done so for the reasons stated.

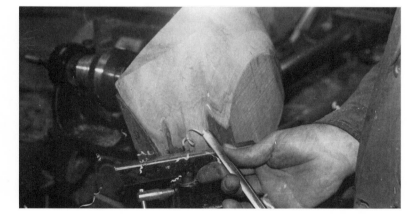

Now fix a faceplate using the centre as a fixing point. If you have a small faceplate, usually with three screw holes, this will be fine. Marking the surface will not matter as this will be the inside of the bowl thus you can use 25mm (1in) or longer screws for safety. I am using a small single screw chuck, fitted with a No. 14 wood screw 32mm (1¼in) long.

Bowl gouges are ground in exactly the same way and to the same shape as the roughing-out gouge but to an angle of about 40°.

Fig. 132. With great care set the tool rest to coincide with the shape of the blank, clamp it tight and give the stuff a turn to ensure it clears. Remember to keep your fingers *your* side of the tool rest all the time. Set the lathe to its slowest speed, approximately 400 rpm, and never attempt work in the square at speeds of above 600 rpm. There will be some vibration as the stuff will be out of balance, but this should not alarm you as long as you take light cuts with a sharp tool and always engage the tool with the work with the handle down low. Let the heel of the bevel rub the work, slowly lifting the handle to take away the shaving. To bring the blank to symmetry as quickly as possible I take a heavy cut using a HSS bowl gouge almost completely on its side and allowing the bevel to rub. Guide the tool around the rough shape being formed so that the cut is made on the left hand, or underside of the gouge. A continuous shaving will not be produced as the blank is not yet a perfect disc. An ordinary LS bowl gouge is used in the same way as the HSS gouge but it will not hold its edge as long. In fact, I completed this bowl with an HSS gouge which was not specially prepared for the purpose and was not sharpened during the entire making. The timber used is hornbeam (*Carpinus betulus*).

Fig. 133. With the blank worked almost to a true disc you may care to try a spindle gouge to effect a finishing cut. I hate to waste timber, and in bowl turning the waste factor is considerable, so I would suggest that instead of taking thick heavy cuts try to use this waste to advantage by using it for practise. I find that the spindle gouge is the tool to use for the final finishing cuts, perhaps because it is a lightweight tool it encourages gentle cuts. It is laid on the revolving stuff with the heel of the bevel contacting the work and the tool precisely placed. The handle is raised to commence the cut which, when working in this direction, must be kept on the left-hand side of the arc shape of the gouge cutting edge.

With the tool rest in line with the shape being formed and below the centre line of the disc, the gouge presented on its side and, taking a light cut, is pushed along the rest raising the handle as necessary to follow the line of working right out to the edge of the blank. Had the blank been carefully prepared in the square prior to mounting at this stage, an interesting finished outside to the bowl would now be almost complete.

Fig. 134.   The outside of the work is continued, working right out to the square section of the blank and progressively reducing it to a true disc. Note the presentation of the tool in this figure, flute up and the cut being made from the side of the cutting edge, making sure the top of the U shape of the tool does not contact, it would do little harm if it did as the action would merely turn the tool away from the work slightly marking the surface at the same time, we will see this angle again in close-up in Fig. 137.

Fig. 135.   The same cut being effected with the tool completely on its side, and as will be seen, the disc is still not perfectly symmetrical. Note the direction of the shaving produced, here it is passing to the left out of the way of the turner and therefore the sight of the working line is not hindered. Either of these methods can be used to bring the work to a perfect disc but it is clear which is best.

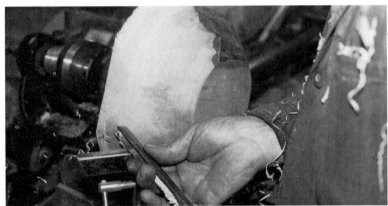

Fig. 136.   The base will require truing up so to avoid unnecessary waste, and to keep the blank as large in overall size as possible, a combination of a few cuts across the base and then a few up the side will eventually join together as a perfect shape. If the blank has an imperfection you wish to remove and doing this would involve a lot of waste, try revising the original design intention. I have often done this and found the result produced a much better style than I had first envisaged. I am using a large 20mm ($\frac{3}{4}$in) spindle gouge with an overhand grip and the side of my hand running along the tool rest is being used to guide the tool along a straight line.

Fig. 137.   When the blank is turned to shape it is time to take a few very fine finishing cuts with the tool flute upwards, right-hand side of the bevel running round the shape for complete control as in Fig. 134. The angle of presentation is maintained in this position all the way from base to periphery, i.e. with the handle down approximately 10–15° from the horizontal. Presented in this way, the cut will be effected just above and to the right of the base of the U shape. Fine cuts will obviate a lot of sanding. You can, of course, make these final cuts with a spindle gouge, I usually do, with the tool presented as discussed in Fig. 133. As the stuff progressively becomes symmetrical the lathe speed can be increased, but for this size, approximately 250mm (10in) diameter, more than 1000 rpm should not be necessary.

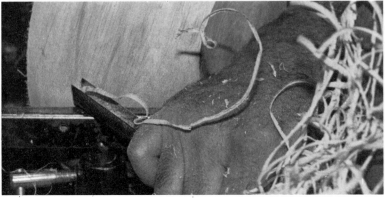

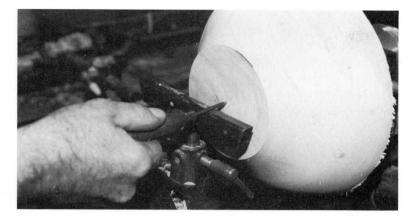

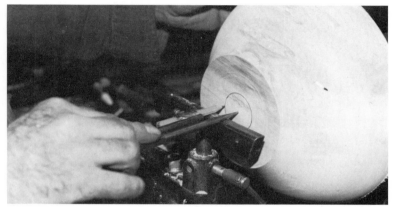

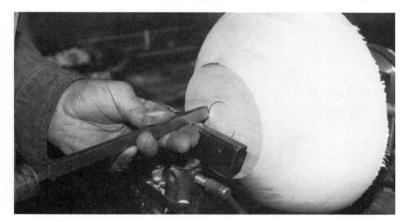

Fig. 138.   We can now decide which method, or which chuck to use to re-mount the work to complete the inside. The choice will be the conventional faceplate fixed with screws; a glue and paper joint using a disc turned true and attached to the base of the blank with adhesive with paper between which can be prised off when the bowl is completed; a rebate worked to accept the expanding collet chuck, see Fig. 224, or as here a spigot chuck of new design by Craft Supplies. I would never recommend a glue and paper joint.

First find the centre using a pointed awl with the lathe running. The speed of the lathe is increased to 1000 rpm or so, and the centre will be 'seen' as the work revolves. Make a light mark with the awl, if the awl does not strike centre it will move in the hand and mark the work. This chuck only requires the ring rebate so the rest of the base area and any marks will show. If this happens it can be remedied by working a dimple after the compass has been used to scribe the 40mm ($1\frac{1}{2}$in) diameter circle required. In fact when the rebate for the chuck is completed and checked for fit, the entire base of the bowl can be decorated, sanded and polished if you wish, as the chuck will not mark it in any way.

Fig. 139.   The tolerance on the precision spigot chuck is minimal, so a 38mm ($1\frac{1}{2}$in) diameter circle must be marked for working. Turn the work by hand to accomplish this.

Fig. 140.   With the long corner of a skew chisel cut a light line dead on the pencil mark, this will produce a clean shoulder for the chuck to grip and give a neat finish.

Fig. 141.   Using a parting tool and working to the previously scribed line, work a rebate approximately 5mm ($\frac{3}{16}$in) deep, keeping the parting tool square with the base of the bowl. Do not try to angle it to produce the required dovetail spigot.

Fig. 142.   It is not really necessary to have a narrow skew chisel for this cut, but as I have one I can make the most of the advantages of this particular chuck. If only a wider tool is available it merely means a wider rebate must be worked to accommodate it. Using only the point or long corner with the tool angled at about 5° and the handle to the left, produce a dovetail-shaped spigot. A precise fit to the shape of the contracting part of the chuck is desirable but not essential, a few trials on scrap wood will soon indicate the required angle. It is interesting to note that when the skew chisel is presented to the work, pointed slightly upwards in a semi-scraping attitude, there is no danger and a clean cut will result. If a scraping tool were presented in this fashion, ground as suggested, it would grab and probably pull the work off the screw chuck, or worse. It is at this time, with the chuck checked for fit and, of course, removed, that any further work in way of decoration to the base can be completed.

Fig. 143.   I will leave the base perfectly flat as I prefer to felt the bases of bowls, then they do not become scratched in use, nor do they damage the furniture upon which they are placed, but it's a matter of choice. The precision spiggot chuck is much the same in principle as an engineers' chuck, in as much as the inside section contracts as the ring is tightened, closing over the worked dowel or spiggot on the object that it is to hold.

Fig. 144.   The chuck is entered into the work and located on the worked spigot. Tighten by hand only, turning the work by hand to see that all is square and adjust if necessary. If you have located properly this will not be required. Gently tighten the chuck with the two C spanners provided, not over-tight, the design of this chuck will not permit over zealousness, nor is it necessary, its gripping power is excellent and positive.

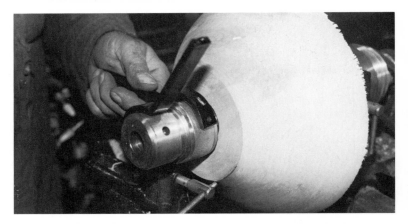

Fig. 145.   With the work reversed, set the tool rest as low as possible, at least 25mm (1in) below the centre line and, with a bowl or spindle gouge, take a couple of light cuts across the face to true up and to remove the rag or spelch occasioned by working the outside. With a skew chisel, long corner down, work a limiting cut approximately 12mm (½in) from the outside edge as in Fig. 140. This will provide a groove to enter the gouge for the preliminary cuts and prevent it skidding off the edge.

Fig. 146.   Over the years I have discovered that no matter how well seasoned timber is, if a bowl is finished in one mounting it will move, however slightly, resulting in an eliptical shape soon after finishing. Of course this can be used to delightful effect, but if a lid is to be fitted, or if you wish to end up with a completely circular bowl, it will have to be worked more than once leaving the time between working dependent on the settlement of the stuff used. It

will also be necessary to re-work the outside as well, and if you have hollowed out the bowl it will only be possible to re-work the outside mounted on the chuck which is not always convenient. For these reasons I work the inside leaving the centre in up to the pencil mark, or perhaps a little less. Then by leaving the workpiece full, say about 25mm (1in) thick, I can set the stuff aside for however long is necessary and re-mount for re-working as often as is required; in some timbers taking a little more off each time until I am satisfied that the stuff has settled down to its new shape.

For the first few cuts let the gouge run in the prepared groove with the bevel rubbing, advance the tool gently to start the cut on its right-hand side. As we are now cutting round a concave shape the full, or almost full, bevel will contact and guide the tool. Note the shaving passing down the flute of the gouge and away, not obscuring the work in any way.

Fig. 147.   The tool in the exact reverse position presented with the bevel rubbing; as the angle of grind is 40°, the handle is not required to be held excessively low. Pull the gouge along the tool rest, square with the work, lifting the handle as necessary to maintain the cut as the shape deepens.

Fig. 148.   If a heavy cut is required the overhand grip may be considered necessary, but note how the waste strikes the hand and builds up around the tool rest making it difficult to see what you are doing, this will mean that you will have to stop cutting to clear it, and if this happens on a finishing cut, which wants to start at the periphery and finish at the centre of the base, this could be a disadvantage.

Fig. 149.   I like to use a spindle gouge for the last few cuts, so when most of the waste is removed, try a little practise with it, and see how you get on. This one is ground at an angle of 45° so it is necessary to hold the handle a little lower to commence the cut, raising it as the shape is followed.

This is a good time to discuss peripheral speed, it's not something to get hung up on, and it has little application in spindle work unless very large diameters are being worked. For bowl work it must be considered as while the speed in revolutions per minute will remain constant, the outside of the work being larger in diameter than the centre will travel further and thus faster. This is confirmed by Fig. 146 and 147 where the pencil marks in the centre are clear and sharp, but the periphery is slightly blurred. Therefore, if you find that you are getting a fine finish, say, from the periphery to the middle, but the middle to the base is a little fuzzy, it may be necessary to stop half way and go up to the next speed to complete the cut. It is also a good reason for starting at a slowish speed and increasing as required. That is all there is to it. See Fig. 150.

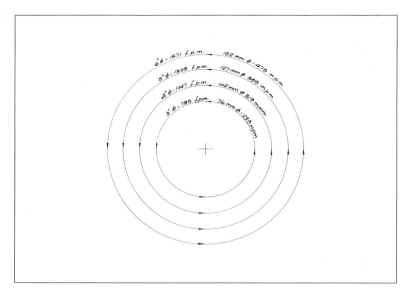

Fig. 150.   Peripheral speeds at 1000 rpm.

Fig. 151.   The same cut using one of the curved rests. They take a little getting used to, and I really prefer to use this type of rest when working with scrapers.

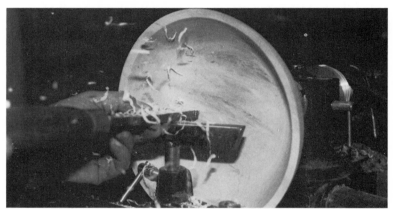

Fig. 152.   A final finish can be obtained with a domed or round-nosed scraper if the shape or depth is such that a cutting tool will not be convenient to use. Keep it very sharp, incline it downwards and take the lightest of cuts. Don't be ashamed to use a scraper, there is a lot to be said for the end justifying the means and on some timbers, when you have had a bit of practise with them, a super finish will result, and anyway why run the risk of wasting or spoiling a nice piece of timber just because it is implied that scraping is not the done thing.

Fig. 153.   From time to time during the hollowing check the depth of the bowl with some sort of gauge. Here I am using the vernier-type caliper. If you don't check, especially towards the completion of the work, you may work right through the base in your enthusiasm. I know, I've done it a time or two and, much to my embarrassment, once at a demonstration!

Fig. 154.   The finished hornbeam bowl is given an overnight soak in Danish oil and left for a week to dry before re-mounting for final polishing. Had it been intended for use as a salad bowl I would have given it several applications of corn or sunflower seed oil until the timber had soaked well before a final polish on the lathe. If you care for garlic in your salad the bowl can be given a good start in life by folding a few cloves in a piece of rag, setting the lathe speed to the slowest and gently pressing the pad on the inside. This will impregnate the timber and permeate the workshop for a day or three as well!

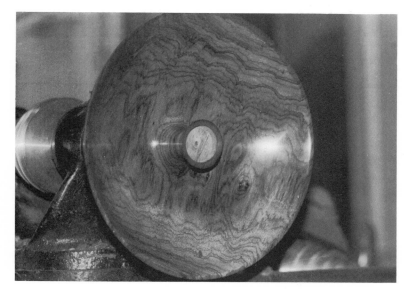

Fig. 155.   A cocobolo bowl with the re-mounting centre left in to re-work a previously rough-turned slab. The centre was then used to form a column upon which to set a smaller bowl on top, see Fig. 157. A shallow rebate is worked in the column, the whole sanded and polished before the top piece is added.

Fig. 156.   A smaller slab in matching timber mounted to enable the outside to be worked. This could, of course, be in a contrasting timber if preferred. The base is then formed to accept both the mini collet chuck to complete the inside and, at the same time, a short spigot to match the rebate in Fig. 155.

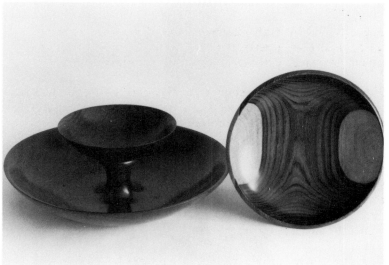

Fig. 157.   On the left is the finished double bowl which is useful for crisps, nuts, etc. On the right is an open bowl illustrating the efficacy of the use of the slab. Made from kingwood (*Dalbergia cerencis*) in which I was lucky enough to find a small log with the cream coloured sapwood intact and in good condition.

Fig. 158.   The pillar or column can be used to support a nut-cracking mechanism. These are available in various styles from turners' suppliers. The one illustrated requires a turned knob to be made to the desired style and in the same or contrasting timber. The bowl and knob illustrated here are in English walnut (*Juglans regia*).

Bud vases

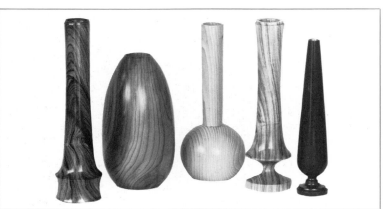

A hobby horse of mine is that the turner does not always require tailor-made material to work with, there are all sorts of things that can be utilised to make exciting and unusual projects and, to this end, the making of bud vases will give me the opportunity to demonstrate this technique.

Fig. 159.   I will be working with a Banksias grandis cone which was sent to me by a turner friend in Australia, where these cones are used for a variety of articles. It is, in effect, a seed pod, and is of a woody nature and I had never even heard of much less seen one. Obviously not everyone will have access to these cones but the techniques I will be using are the same for conventional timber and bud vases make an ideal project to commence with as they can be completed with the minimum of timber.

Fig. 160.   A variety of shapes and timbers; from left to right are cocobolo (*Dalbergia retusa*) with a cigar tube used for the insert; Australian apricot (*Prunus armeniaca*) with a proprietary glass insert; Yew (*Taxus baccata*) with a copper pipe suitably plugged to make it watertight, and shaped at the top to make it look tidy; Brazilian tulipwood (*Dalbergia frutescens*) with a cigar tube insert, and finally African blackwood (*Dalbergia melonoxylon*) and, as this shape was required to taper to a fine top section, the insert was made up from a length of 10mm ($\frac{3}{8}$in) copper pipe, plugged and with the top shaped to effect a neat finish. This project will give some experience in drilling on the lathe itself although this is not the only method used to hollow out the vase.

Fig. 161.   The cone was not a particularly difficult shape to deal with, to start I had to produce a flat at both ends to facilitate mounting between centres as you would if using a conventional piece of stuff.

Fig. 162.   This was accomplished with a tenon saw and it was then that I discovered just how hard the material was. The cut gave me the opportunity to study the structure of the cone. It was formed with three distinct layers. The first skin or bark, was quite soft and easy to work, then a thin layer of fur and finally the core of a hard substance, cork-like in appearance.

Fig. 163.   As the cone was reasonably symmetrical it was not difficult to find the centres of the two ends, these centres were drilled to accept the drive and dead (tailstock) centres. The cone was mounted between centres and a 25mm (1 in) dowel or spigot was worked at the headstock end, see Fig. 301, to enable the work to be supported at one end only for drilling the hole that is required for the insert. For some applications it is sometimes a distinct advantage to have the stuff mounted off-centre, as interesting and unusual configurations can result due to a part or section of the material being left in its natural state.

I decided to complete the drilling first, and an engineer's geared chuck was mounted in the tailstock, see Fig. 287, into which was fitted a 25mm (1in) machine auger. This is the diameter required for the glass insert which is made just undersize to fit a 25mm (1 in) hole. When fitting any drill into an engineer's chuck remember to nip not crush with the chuck key, progressively tightening all three jaws by fitting the key into the three holes provided. This action will not only centre the drill perfectly, but you will find that after the first hole is tightened to its fullest extent, a slight turn will be possible on the second and then the third.

With the cone thus mounted, and the auger set up as described, it was advanced to just contact the indent in the cone left by the dead centre, this will ensure perfect placement prior to switching on the lathe.

Fig. 164.   Most drill chucks fix into the tailstock by means of a morse taper. It is, therefore, wise to hold the chuck to prevent any tendency for it to revolve with the work. Select a low speed for this diameter drill, not more than 500 rpm, and preferably slower. Keep the drill cutting and advance it into the work slowly and gently. It will be necessary with metal drills to wind the drill out occasionally to clear the shavings. If you don't, they will build up inside the hole and create unnecessary heat, expanding the drill and doing no good to its temper, or yours for that matter.

Fig. 165.   The size of drill must be selected to accommodate the insert and it sounds silly but do remember that an *exact* 25mm (1in) dowel will not fit into an *exact* 25mm (1in) hole. Glass will not stand too much pushing and pulling so make up a replica in timber and when this fits without problem and can easily be withdrawn, the glass fitting can be inserted. I feel this type of insert looks best positioned just below the rim of the vase.

Fig. 166.   The glass insert offered up to make a final test fit and then set safely aside, and not where a nice heavy tool can inadvertently be placed on it!

Fig. 167.   Replace the replica in the hole and bring the tailstock up to support the work, I am using an interchangeable revolving or live tailstock centre, which is looked at it in detail in Fig. 202. Supported thus, turning to shape can commence. I had made a sketch of an antique leather bottle and thought this Banksias cone would be an excellent medium in which to try to reproduce it. With a spindle gouge, and making sure I kept my knuckles away from those pods, I started the first few cuts at 1500 rpm. I only had one cone so I did not want to make any mistakes. The outer layer worked with ease and the fur can be seen revealed. It is the dark area, in the picture and is much like heavy velour in texture and depth.

Fig. 168.   I continued working into the core and found whilst hard it was no problem and was not in danger of falling to pieces. The next thing to find out was how it would sand and finish. I decided to work the neck of the bottle to a finish and try one of the friction polishes such as Craftlac. I now knew the material would accept the gouge so I tried the chisel, and this provided a splendid finish requiring only the minimum of sanding. Two coats of polish were applied at intervals of about ten minutes, fined down with 0000 gauge steel wool and given a final polish with the lathe running and using the smallest quantity of polish. The effect can be seen in Fig. 159.

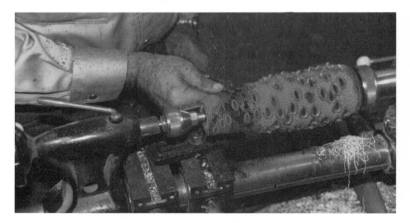

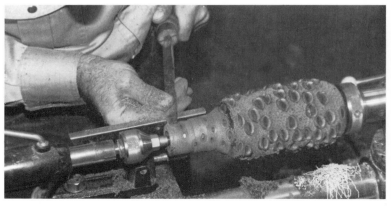

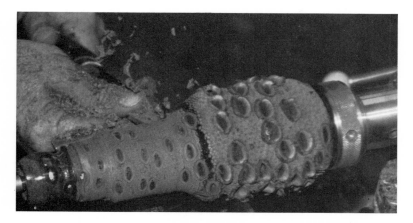

Fig. 169.   As I was working, or shall we say experimenting, on the extreme end of the stuff, if anything had gone wrong it could have been removed by parting off and no more harm than a shortening of the cone would have resulted. Returning to the spindle gouge, the rest of the design shape was completed, and the work sanded.

Fig. 170.   Before polishing, a few seeds were poked out of the pods with the point of an awl. The work can then be parted off using a narrow parting tool and finally a tenon saw to complete.

Fig. 171.   An alternate method of mounting would be to effect the drilling in the drill press and using the same chuck body, but mounted complete with a pin mandrel, see Fig. 305 for details, the vase can be produced the other way round. If you wish to use an insert of unconventional type you can make up your own mandrel mounted on a screw chuck, see Fig. 312 and 313. Both these methods will permit the vase to be completed and finished all round, including polishing the base if you wish. They also facilitate re-mounting the work for a progressive finishing process such as would be required if using varnish or plastic coating which would necessitate re-mounting to flat down between coats, and for final burnishing.

Fig. 172.   While glass inserts are ideal I find the standard size to be restrictive, and they cannot easily be cut. I have found there is a wealth of throw-away objects that can be used to excellent effect and, if you wish, you can glue in the insert to make it permanent. A selection of such inserts include patent medicine tubes in plastic or aluminium, cigar tubes, odd lengths of copper pipe, etc. In the background is a small jig I use to hold the copper pipe while I dress the top to some sort of shape using a boxwood punch turned on the lathe. A plug will be required to stop the base of pipes and should preferably be made from teak, iroko or other oily, impervious to water, timber.

Corn cob holders

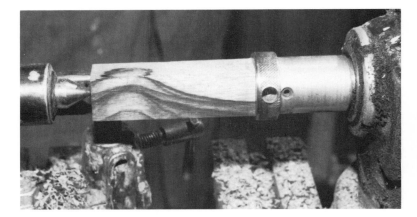

Small pieces of timber that the turner accumulates over the years should never, ever be thrown away, however small. These are but two of the many useful articles that can be produced and the method can be extended to making all sorts of small objects such as, knobs, thimbles, drawstring toggles for anoraks and wooden jewellery.

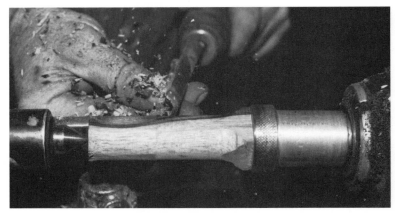

Fig. 173.   Starting with corn cob holders I shall describe two methods of completing them. For the style with its own spike I selected a small piece of Macassar ebony (*Diopyros*) of half and half heart and sapwood. The steel spiked design shown here is in Brazilwood (*Caesalpinia echinata*), sometimes called Pernambuco.

Fig. 174.   A piece of 20mm (¾in) square by 75mm (3in) long will be ample. Approximately 20mm (¾in) should be allowed for waste as it is mounted in a screw chuck, and the stuff should be drilled to this depth.

Fig. 175.   Work down to a cylinder but leave a square section at the screw chuck end. This will enable you to use a spanner to remove the work easily from the chuck and, as we will need to re-mount it once or twice for finishing, this is necessary.

Fig. 176.   With a pencil lay off any design marks required, using a rule, a pre-prepared template or profile gauge.

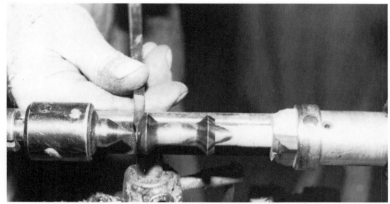

Fig. 177.   With a parting tool reduce the stuff down, in this case the centre is approximately 10mm ($\frac{3}{8}$in) diameter. Continue to the chuck end in like manner or use a narrow gouge, this section needs to be left full as it will be required to take some strain in the working of the handle and in the final finishing.

Fig. 178.   Work the handle to the design shape, and draw the tailstock away from the work, this will enable the end to be finished with a gouge or, as here with a skew chisel, long corner down. Take fine cuts to remove the mark in the work left by the centre.

Fig. 179.   The cut, shown in close-up, can also be effected with the centre supporting the work but take care not to foul the gouge in the process. Take cuts almost up to the centre, enough to complete with one final slice.

Fig. 180.   Various finishes can be used bearing in mind the use of the object. One of my favourites for this sort of article is plastic coating, made by Rustins and readily available at hardware stores. It comes as a complete pack of varnish, catalyst hardener, thinner and burnishing cream. The varnish is mixed as per the instructions in the pack. Its life, once mixed with catalyst, is limited as with all two-pack products, but I find that storing in the refrigerator, clearly labelled of course, will render the mixture usable for at least four or five days. Its great advantage is that once a good foundation of finish is applied, even if it is contaminated with dust specks, brush marks, etc, it can be cleaned up with 0000 gauge steel wool and then brought back to a brilliant lustre by application of the burnishing cream. As I dislike cleaning paint brushes I find that small objects like this respond well to dipping. Here we have the mixture prepared in a suitable container and the holder, having been dipped, can be allowed to drain for a few moments and then given a flick, much as you would a thermometer, to remove any excess and set aside to dry. It is as well to do this in a cool place as curing of the mixture is accelerated by heat.

Fig. 181. I find that about three dips at intervals of about three hours will fill the grain even on porous timbers and leave a thickness of varnish sufficient to re-mount on the lathe for flatting with either 350 garnet if it is a bit lumpy, or 0000 gauge steel wool. One final dip for a perfect finish and then allow it to cure for at least three days and preferably seven. By this time the finish is at its hardest, and by returning the work to the lathe the burnishing cream will be all that is necessary to finally flat and produce a superb shine. The rag with which the burnishing cream is applied should be kept well moistened with water. Note: The addition of 10% extra hardener to the mix will give a harder finish, particularly suitable for lathe polishing. Finish by polishing with a soft cloth after application of the burnishing cream. For an extra super shine, metal polish can be used as a final polishing medium.

Fig. 182. With the handle completed and polished we now have the job of finishing off the spike and parting off. Take the parting tool and working as before, reduce the spike section to a taper with a diameter of approximately 4mm ($\frac{3}{16}$in) at the handle end. Before turning the parting tool over slightly to the left to effect the parting, sand the spike to a fine finish. As this is the part that will enter the cob no other finish is necessary.

Fig. 183. The finished holder, note the small shoulder where the spike joins the handle. Prior to using the parting tool, if a light nick is made with the point of the skew chisel to leave a clean line at this point, it will protect the handle from damage during the finishing of the spike.

Fig. 184. An alternative method uses an even shorter piece of timber to make the handle on a prepared mandrel and then something like a pop rivet is fitted to form the spike. Cross mark a piece of stuff for the mandrel and set it up in the screw chuck. This time, as we will be working close to the prepared mandrel it must be turned perfectly cylindrical to avoid any danger of knuckle-rapping. A washer of fibre-board or ply will permit working up to the chuck but not touching it. Work the mandrel to a shape that will permit the turning of the handle to be effected all round, and produce a spigot of a diameter that will match the diameter of the pop rivet. The end of the spigot acts as a guide i.e. the shoulder of the spigot is the same diameter as the part of the rivet that will be exposed when in position in the handle.

Cross mark and drill a hole deep enough to accommodate the shank of the rivet in the stuff to be used for the holder.

Fig. 185.   Slip the work on to the mandrel and bring the tailstock up to support it during the working.

Fig. 186.   Complete the turning as before taking special care when finishing across the tailstock end, especially if you have been as clumsy as I have been and nicked the shoulder of the mandrel, Fig. 187. It may be necessary to work as shown in Fig. 178 and 179 leaving the small pip at the end to be removed with a sharp knife on the bench.

Fig. 187.   With the turning completed and sanded to a fine finish insert the rivet and with the rivetting tool, and the lightest of squeezes or you will split the stuff, expand the rivet slightly. If you put a little blob of Araldite epoxy resin in the hole before inserting the rivet, nothing will ever pull it out. Allow the adhesive to cure for about seven days and then it will be a simple matter to beat the end to an awl shape to permit ease of entry into the cob and prevent it twisting in use. The pin part of pop rivets are of necessity soft and usually of a monel type metal i.e. resistant to rust.

I find that a plastic container of Danish oil is a very useful thing to have handy. Small objects can be popped in and left for a day or so to soak up the oil, allowed to dry and then, either on the lathe (it would be a simple matter to make up another mandrel to accept the spike), or with a cloth, give a final polish. The container must have a tight-fitting lid to prevent evaporation of the expensive Danish oil.

Fig. 188.   To make a small stand for the holders really completes the job. The making of the stand will be an adaptation of the methods we will discuss when we come to the sandglasses page 118. The holders here are all the same shape, but in four pairs of different timbers. Lignum vitae (*Guaiacum officinale*), Rio rosewood (*Dalbergia nigra*), Greenheart (*Ocotia rodiaei*), Kingwood (*Dalbergia cirensis*). The stand is in Indian rosewood (*Dalbergia latifolia*).

Light pulls and knobs

Fig. 189. Most houses have a few corded light pulls, usually made in white plastic. A few minutes work and with the minimum of timber can alter all that and for this example I have used a piece of olivewood (*Olea*).

Fig. 190. Start the work in exactly the same way as for the cob holder with metal spike, but this time as the section is larger make the spigot on the mandrel a little longer than the depth of the hole in the work. A diameter of 8mm ($\frac{5}{16}$in) is usually suitable to accommodate the knot in the cord and 12mm ($\frac{1}{2}$in) deep is ample, and this will leave room to fit a finishing plug in the base to hide the knotted cord.

Fig. 191. With the work mounted in this mandrel and supported by the tailstock mark out and work to a rough finished shape. As the spigot of the mandrel is longer than the hole in the workpiece it will be easy to work all round and, just as important, to be able to finish all round should you wish to apply plastic coating or similar.

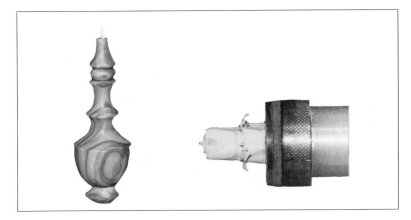

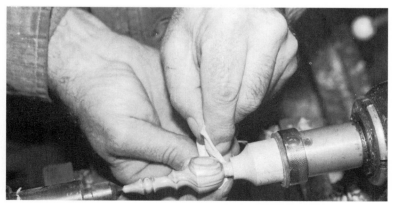

Fig. 192. Place a Jacob's chuck in the tailstock and with a drill of approximately 3mm ($\frac{1}{8}$in) diameter drill right through. Withdraw the drill at intervals to clear the waste or it will heat up, expand, and turn the stuff on the mandrel, which will spoil the nice snug fit you have prepared. You will probably want to use the mandrel to make several of these pulls while you are at it.

Fig. 193. Complete the turning and then take a very sharp skew chisel, and with the long corner down, the tool pointing into the waste and keeping away from the steel of the centre, use the lightest of cuts to work a neat finish to the tailstock end. A drop of linseed oil on the dead centre will ensure it does not burn or squeak.

Fig. 194. Bring the tailstock up to just touch, too much pressure might split the fine section of stuff, to give sufficient support to the work and keep it tight on the mandrel. Sand carefully with garnet or similar paper taking care not to damage the profiles you have worked, and always sand or polish with one hand supported by the other for safety.

Fig. 195. The final polish in close-up. Even on small items like this let one hand support the other, and work as far as possible in such a position that if the cloth or paper is snatched out of your grasp it will disappear *away* from you. By withdrawing the tailstock it is obvious that this article can be removed and remounted as often as you wish, for a progressive finishing process.

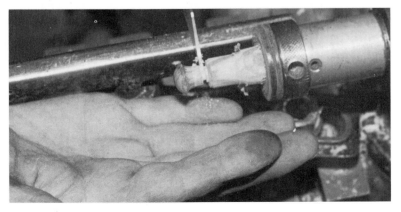

Fig. 196.   While the commercially produced light pull is open-ended, we have the facility to make a really up-market job and to this end, a small piece of the same or contrasting timber set up in the screw chuck to make a finial or pip to completely cover the open end will give a fine finish. Support the stuff with the tailstock and work the end almost to a finish. Produce a dowel to fit the hole in the base of the pull using calipers or vernier. Note my thumb resting on the screw to prevent vibration moving it and thus altering from the set size.

Fig. 197.   I am using a home-made parting tool that was ground down from a length of tool steel by an engineer friend, to approximately 2mm ($\frac{1}{16}$in) width. This is ideal for this sort of work as the short length of stuff will allow about three pips to be made from one mounting. With the tool a little on its side, work a fine chamfer to permit easy entry of the pip into the pull.

Fig. 198.   With a skew chisel, long corner down, remove the mark made by the centre, then sand and polish to finish.

Fig. 199.   With the pip completed take the narrowest parting tool you have and part off, placing your hand under the work to catch it as it falls, if tiny things like this fall into the shavings under the lathe, they can be most vexing to find!

Lids

We live in a frighteningly throw-away society and in an effort to make us buy their products, manufacturers pack them in a variety of jars and pots, most of which we can, with the aid of some of the accessories that are now available from turners' supplies, re-cycle and make into attractive and useful containers. There are lots of ways to make plain wooden lids and there are plenty of methods of decorating them to enable their use at the table, here are but a few.

Fig. 200.   If you feel up to a bit of repetition work this is a spice rack that will be welcomed by any cook, using a well-known brand of spice container that can be found in every supermarket. On the right, and using containers of different styles and sizes, the method is adapted to produce a condiment set for the table.

Fig. 201.   A variety of containers with plain lids or lids with tile or enamelled inserts. Some containers with glass lids can be embellished. All that these items require is a very small quantity of stuff and time spent in the workshop.

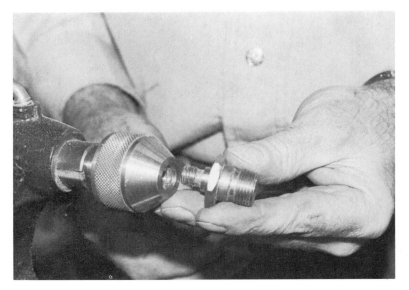

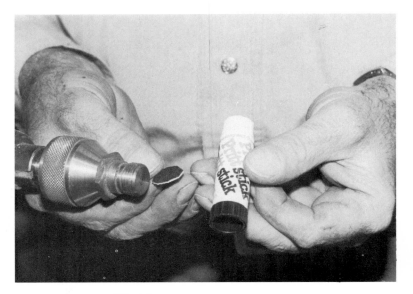

Fig. 202.   There is a relatively new accessory available that I find very useful and for this type of work is invaluable. It is the interchangeable revolving centre and this one is manufactured by Coronet, so let's have a look at its functions. Basically it is a normal live or revolving centre, into which can be screwed a part which I will call the pusher, we will see why in a moment.

Fig. 203.   With the pusher in place an attachment can be threaded on in the form of a cone chuck, and this will be found very convenient to use in situations where marking of the tailstock end of the work is to be avoided, such as split turnings, etc.

Fig. 204.   Reverting to the pusher, a leather washer can be made and temporarily glued into place with an easily soluble adhesive and used as a steady to hold work on a false faceplate mandrel, see Fig. 214, with no fear of marking the finished surface.

Fig. 205.   Fitted with a normal centre.

Fig. 206.   Fitted with a ring or cup centre.

Fig. 207.   Let us start by making a few identical lids, six in line, and with the stuff set up in the 6-in-1 chuck. It is unlikely that you will have a sawtooth bit that will exactly fit the diameter of the metal lid, but at least some of the waste can be removed with the drill, marked with masking tape to control the depth of cut. The stuff is divided into the six sections and a parting tool used to make cuts to a depth of about 6mm ($\frac{1}{4}$in) and then the final diameter of the cylinder turned to size. Worked in that order if there is any spelch from the parting tool, the final sizing will eradicate it.

Fig. 208.   The final fit can be worked with the long corner of the skew chisel, the finish to the inside is not important, in fact to help grip the lid it won't hurt to be a little rough.

Fig. 209.   Check the diameter with a vernier with the lathe stopped or with outside calipers with the lathe running.

Fig. 210.   A final test of the lid with the jar attached. This will enable you to remove the lid easily especially if the design calls for a deep insert.

Fig. 211.   Satisfied with the fit the first lid can be parted off with a parting tool, to conserve timber use the narrowest tool you have. Continue with the same method for all six, keeping the lids matched to the metal lids by numbering the inside of the work and scratching the corresponding number or letter on the paint of the metal lid. Metal lids are not all exactly the same size, so this will save some vexation later, especially if you are working to fine limits.

Fig. 212.   The last small piece of stuff in the chuck can now be used as a mandrel for the lids. Work the waste piece to a snug fit, (if there has been much variance with the size of the metal lids, start with the largest).

Fig. 213.   Slip the lid on, and the rough finish from the parting tool can now be removed. If one of the new hollow ground parting tools has been used, little more than sanding will be required and if the finish is a little rough, a square-across scraper will sort it out. As the action will be one of working towards the stuff on the mandrel, there will be no fear of the work twisting off.

Fig. 214. Alternatively, the lids can be fitted to the metal insert as previously discussed, felled off, and the rest of the shaping on the top, can be completed on the mandrel. Then, by bringing up the pusher complete with the leather or rubber washer, to support, it can be used to maintain the work in position while any detail on the remainder of the lid is completed. The lid can be sanded and polished on the mandrel and can, of course, be replaced as many times as is necessary. If a number of this size lid is to be made at different times, the prepared mandrel can be removed from the chuck and replaced later when more lids are required.

Fig. 215. It is not necessary to have long lengths of stuff available and one of the many ways to use those little pieces of stuff that quickly accumulate is to make individual lids. With the stuff mounted in a screw chuck, with a *short* screw, turn to a disc. Work the required rebate in the top to accommodate the expanding collet-type fixing, see Fig. 223. The entire top and outside of the lid can be finished and polished, including the rebate, as the collet won't mark it if it is mounted with care.

Fig. 216. The rest of the work on the lid can be done with the stuff reversed on the collet chuck as previously discussed. The collet rebate can then be removed by reversing the stuff, again on a prepared mandrel as in Fig. 214 or, if you prefer cut a disc from a piece of leather to fit into the collet rebate. This can produce a delightful effect as in the small 'lighthouse' jar lid in Fig. 200. You can also insert this type of finish into the bases of bowls that have been worked with the collet chuck method. I once heard a customer say, among other complimentary things 'look, he even goes to the trouble of fitting a little leather disc into the bottom', and it is these little touches which effect a pleasing finish.

Fig. 217. When making racks or stands as in Fig. 200 to fit or to contain the jars it is again unlikely that you will have the precise size drill to work the necessary hole for the jar. In the long spice rack it would be exciting to say the least to work the required holes on the lathe! It would be akin to facing a cavalry charge – on the end hole, anyway. It is sometimes more convenient to make the base fitting and then place it where it is wanted. The method is similar to making the lids except that for this application the inside will be seen, so this is this area to work to a finish.

Fig. 218.   The outside part that will be visible in the finished piece can also be shaped, sanded and polished. A shallow dowel is worked on the base to the size that will fit one of your existing drills.

Fig. 219.   The finished base parted off and ready to be placed into position in the pre-drilled stand.

Fig. 220.   Turning the 'lighthouse' pillar for the square-based stand. The top section was worked with the stuff secured in the 6-in-1 chuck. The whole pillar could have

been completed in the 6-in-1 but to cut out waste it was then removed and set up between centres with the top supported by the revolving centre. This will mark the inside so work a disc to fit and thus protect it.

Lids with decorative inserts

Fig. 221.   Among the accessories to the 6-in-1 chuck are the expanding collets in sizes from 20 mm ($\frac{3}{4}$in) diameter, known as mini-expanding collets up to 90mm ($3\frac{1}{2}$in) for large bowls. The principle of working the fitting rebate is the same for all. The action of the chuck is to expand the four jaws of the dovetail-shaped collets to hold the work positively and to permit precise replacement of the work if, for any reason, it is found necessary to remove it from the chuck and later replace it, for instance for a progressive finishing process. The body of the chuck is fitted with the shaped centre boss, and a larger size is used for collets greater in diameter than the 20mm ($\frac{3}{4}$in) and 32mm ($1\frac{1}{4}$in).

Fig. 222.   The tightening ring has the effect of pulling the collet back into the chuck and, in so doing, expanding the dovetail-shaped ring, shown in Fig. 223.

Fig. 223.   With the ring in place the work, in this case with a rebate of 20mm ($\frac{3}{4}$in) diameter, is placed over the collet indicated with the pencil and the ring tightened with the C spanners provided with the chuck. The elastic band while not exactly standard engineering practice is merely to keep the four separate parts of the assembly together for the convenience of fitting them into the chuck, they have no other use but for this reason should not be removed.

Fig. 224.   Here the chuck is fitted with the largest-size expanding collet. There are several sizes with rings that fit the collets perfectly and can be screwed to the base of a bowl blank, should you wish to do so.

Fig. 225.   Let us then discuss a few other methods of making lids for jars, this time a more decorative type. On a screw chuck the stuff is worked to a disc. I am using a short-ground beading tool placed on the work and bevel rubbing approximately 3mm ($\frac{1}{8}$in) in from either side. The handle is lifted to commence the cut and then the tool is drawn sideways across the face of the workpiece. The tool is kept square with the surface all the time. A spindle gouge could be also used for this work.

Fig. 226. The heavy scraper ground straight across is used to effect a flat surface square with the sides. Take light cuts and keep the tool inclined down all the time. Some people find it best to commence with the tool to the right of the centre vertical line, i.e. where the work is revolving *upwards*, and the tool is rubbing against the stuff. Then by drawing it to the left as it crosses the vertical centre point, i.e. where the work is revolving *downwards*, the cut can start. Try to keep the tool cutting on the horizontal centre line as this will prevent the little pip forming at the centre.

Fig. 227. There are several choices of decorative insert. We can fit one of the many ceramic tile designs that are available, as shown here or an enamelled disc, or work a rebate to accommodate a picture to be covered by glass with a separate ring to secure it, or any other ideas that come to mind. For any of these methods, once the rebate is worked, the fitting rebate for the mini-collet can be produced. While the collet shape will indicate that a precise matching rebate is required in the workpiece, I have found in practice this is quite unnecessary, in fact, for small work like this, a Forstner or sawtooth bit will produce the required hole and 3mm ($\frac{1}{8}$in) deep is more than ample.

Fig. 228. Working the collet rebate with a narrow skew chisel. If you wish, the hole can be matched to the collet shape to some extent by moving the tool handle to the right. This will have some decorative effect if the hole is to be left in as a design, or it can be filled with a disc of some sort, but it is not necessary, in any event don't overdo it as excessive angle will diminish the holding power of the chuck.

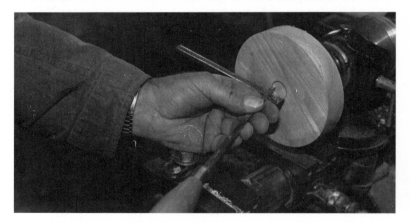

Fig. 229. With the very small diameter collets I find that a perfectly precise placement can be effected by hand tightening the ring only. Bring up the tailstock, either with the pusher or just the tailstock itself to exert light pressure dead centre, then give a turn or two and the disc will revolve true with no oscillation. Finally nip up gently with the C spanners.

Fig. 230. Using the vernier to establish the outside diameter.

Fig. 231. For this exercise the decorative top of the glass lid shows through the timber surround, so a second diameter must be measured, in this instance the area of the glass lid up to the upstand. As this area will be used to glue the two parts, it must be prepared with care. If a set of these jars are to be made, the depth should be consistent and this can be measured with the depth gauge of the vernier.

Fig. 232. The waste can be removed quickly with a scraper or a skew chisel, having first used the long corner of the skew to cut a clean line on the marks.

Fig. 233. With the rebate prepared to the required depth and diameter, some of the centre waste is removed, but not too much it will be quite easy to remove the remainder later.

Fig. 234.   This type of lid is usually a glass casting and they are not precise nor always completely circular. As we will be attaching glass, which is inert, to timber which is not, a little free play will be required, so test with the lid.

Fig. 235.   At this stage it is a good time to offer up the whole jar and see if any design styles come to mind and to check the balance of timber to glass from a design point of view. Obviously this work requires reducing in both size and style to balance with the size of the container. Such shaping can be started now or later, as you wish.

Fig. 236.   Mount a piece of scrap timber or ply on a screw chuck or small faceplate and work to a diameter that will snugly fit the rebate worked for the glass lid.

Fig. 237.   Remove the workpiece from the mini-collet and set up on this prepared mandrel, original side out. Any further detail or decoration can be worked, or the tile or whatever inserted.

Fig. 238.   Alternatively, taking a parting tool and working to a measured diameter, the waste from the centre of the workpiece can be removed. By taking the minimum of waste out of the centre it will be seen that a very usable section of stuff can be retained. This is worth saving if it is a piece of valuable or rare timber. There is no fear of going in too far with the parting tool as there is a wooden plate behind the work so no damage to the tool will result. In fact it will be clear at this stage that while we have been engaged in the making of a lid we have covered the production of small picture frames as well.

Fig. 239.   With the centre removed, and the final details worked, the lid or frame can be sanded and polished, this mandrel will permit the work to be replaced as many times as is necessary to effect whatever finish is chosen.

Fig. 240.   The finished lid is shown on the left, and another design is mounted on the mandrel for final polishing. Scuff the glass around the outer ring to obtain a key for the adhesive. I would use one of the silicone caulks available, such as Clam as it is flexible and will tolerate any slight movement of the timber. Only the lightest touch of adhesive is required and any excess removed while it is soft.

Metal lids can also be sanded with garnet paper in the same way as glass lids and set into the timber with an epoxy resin adhesive such as Araldite.

Nutcrackers

These make an interesting progression from the previous projects as they involve both spindle and faceplate work, combined with the manufacture of a home-made jig should you wish to do so. They will tax your ability to work to reasonably fine limits. As woodworkers we are fortunate in our ability to make things we want in the material we like and in the style that pleases us, Nutcrackers are available in the shops but usually in one design only, made in beech and in such sizes that a cob nut will escape to the side of the screw, too small to accommodate a Californian walnut and not of sufficient strength to crack a Brazil nut.

Fig. 241. From left to right top row shows the nutcracker described in this chapter made from Canadian rock maple, Cocobolo, English walnut, all with a bore of at least 45mm ($1\frac{3}{4}$in). The egg-cup style with the musical instrument key

screw with a thread diameter of 12mm ($\frac{1}{2}$in) is in pearwood with a bore of 30mm ($1\frac{1}{8}$in) which is ideal for cob nuts, pecans, almonds, etc. Along the bottom row we have Israeli olivewood, spalted (that is diseased) but in use for some considerable time; then one of those timbers which is almost extinct in the market, Ziricote or Grand'e Palisander (*Cordia dodecandra*). It is sometimes referred to as Mexican rosewood, it comes from Mexico but is not botanically a Dalbergia. The final two are made from English boxwood, perfect for the purpose but not the most exciting timber in way of appearance, other than its rather ivory yellow colour. To sum up, any close-grain hardwood will suffice and sycamore, holly and fruitwoods are ideal, have a delightful colour and grain, not to mention the tensile strength required.

Thread boxes will deal with most timbers and the taps

will, in my experience, work all but the exceptionally hard such as lignum vitae. If, for instance, it was decided to make a cracker in ebony, the tap would work the female thread in the body with ease, but for the screw it would, perhaps, be prudent to make the thread in beech, soak it for an hour or so in spirit black and then let it into an ebony handle using the method described in Fig. 266–269. The techniques and methods discussed in making nutcrackers, will have many other applications and uses, and the investment in one or two sizes of thread box is well worth the expense.

Fig. 242.   Take a block 65mm (2½in) square by 55mm (2¼) long and accurately mark in the diagonals. Then with a try square mark for drilling. The marked part of the block will be the opening of the cracker, thus the hole for threading will be approximately 22mm ($\frac{7}{8}$in) from this part to place the screw at a position just above the centre line of the depth to prevent nuts being squeezed out under pressure.

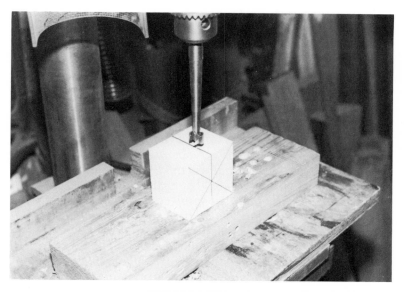

Fig. 243.   Starting the threads is not always easy, especially in hardwood. I have found that it is best to fix the tap in the drill press, cramp or hold the work with one hand, apply light pressure, with my chin, on the press handle, and start the first turn of the tap using the chuck key as a tommybar. This will start the thread true.
    Drill a 15mm ($\frac{5}{8}$in) hole for the $\frac{3}{4}$in thread about half-way through the block, ensure it is dead centre. Drill for the screw chuck, again with care to ensure centricity, on the marked end, either now or after threading.

Fig. 244.   Remove the work from the drill press *without* removing the tap from the work and finish with a wrench in the normal way. Note: When using either the tap or the die, use plenty of lubricant such as linseed oil. This can be removed later with white spirit and will cause no polishing problems. Depending on the timber used, generally it is not wise to back the tap or die after each turn, as when working steel; complete the thread in one direction only, to approximately half-way through the block.

Fig. 245. With the work mounted on a screw chuck, using either a spindle or roughing-out gouge, turn to a cylinder at a speed of approximately 1500 rpm, but do not work to the final size at this stage. The work can be supported with the tailstock, as this will prevent any likelihood of the screw stripping. There is no danger in working stuff with a hole in it, but a little extra care, especially when sanding, to let the fingers trail will not go amiss. There is no fear whatsoever of the tool catching in the hole.

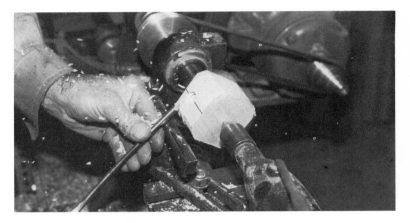

Fig. 246. Bring the rest across the base and using a skew chisel at the same speed work the collet chuck recess (25mm (1in) for the Coronet mini-collet) to a depth of 3mm ($\frac{1}{8}$in). Finish with the chisel skewed to work the base of the recess flat and clean. The entire base can now be sanded and polished, including the collet recess, as the action of the collet will not damage the polish. Alternatively, the recess can be finished later with a leather washer. It is also possible to make up a mandrel similar to Fig. 270 to fix the finished work on and thus complete the work with a perfectly flat base.

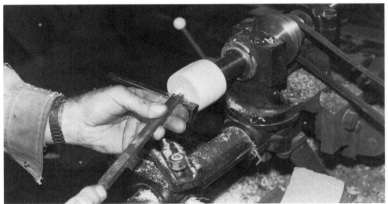

Fig. 247. The body of the cracker is now reversed and mounted on the mini-collet. I find that a little pressure from the tailstock as I tighten the collect chuck ensures the work is mounted true. The alternative collet chuck is the 6-in-1, it has the advantage of two sizes 20mm ($\frac{3}{4}$in) and 28mm ($1\frac{1}{8}$in) and the tolerance in way of hole diameter size is considerably greater which is useful if you wish to insert decorative items like coins in the collet hole.

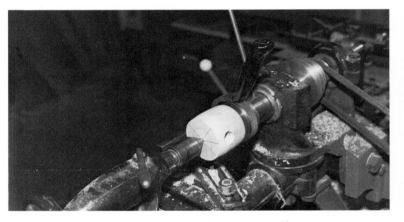

Fig. 248. The central hole size will, of course, vary, but for a general purpose nutcracker a diameter of 40mm ($1\frac{5}{8}$in) and a depth of 48mm ($1\frac{7}{8}$m) is ideal. A barrel shape will keep the thickness of timber at the threaded part where it is most needed. Or, depending on the design, at the thickest parts such as a bead. Most, if not all the waste, can be removed with a drill, preferably using a sawtooth bit, but by boring with any available drill the remainder of the waste can speedily be removed with the very sharp long corner of a skew chisel.

Fig. 249. Set the tool rest at a height that will permit the point of the skew to enter the work dead centre, i.e. the rest height will be *half* the thickness of the chisel used below the centre line. Take light cuts, no more than 2mm ($\frac{1}{16}$in) at a time, keeping the skew horizontal and square with the direction of cut. Remember that this will in fact effect an overall diameter reduction of 4mm ($\frac{1}{8}$in) at each cut. Keep the point sharp and at the finish of the cut push the handle to the right to keep the bottom clean and tidy. This is a semi-scraping action, but with close-grain hardwoods will produce a shaving, albeit fine, and will not dull the tool unduly. The final cut is made with a newly-sharpened tool taking the lightest of cuts to render a finish that will need the minimum of sanding.

Fig. 250. The body finished, sanded and polished. I do not apply any polish to the inside as this will become scratched in use and look most unsightly, instead sander sealer well cut down with 000 gauge steel wool is all the finish required.

Fig. 251. For the screw, a piece of timber 40mm ($1\frac{1}{2}$in) section by some 100mm (4in) long is mounted between centres and turned to a cylinder. The handle end is to the headstock and from the headstock mark approximately 32mm ($1\frac{1}{4}$in). With a parting tool at a speed of 1500 rpm and using a vernier or calipers, reduce the work to a diameter of 20mm ($\frac{3}{4}$in). Make two or three more cuts the same way along the length.

Fig. 252. With a roughing gouge canted over as shown, and working from left to right remove the waste down to the parting tool depths, leaving just a touch full. Note plenty of tool rest at the tailstock end to avoid the tool falling off which can be most painful on the forefinger, as it is forced down on the tool rest holder.

Fig. 253.   The part to be threaded can now be worked to a true 20mm ($\frac{3}{4}$in) diameter, in fact just fine of this to enable the work to slip through the thread box (die) smoothly. The skew chisel is the tool for this job. Check constantly with the vernier as the size is important, too small will render a sloppy fitting in the body, too tight and it will not pass through the die or dislodge the die cutter, or both. Work a slight taper at the tailstock end to facilitate easy entry into the die.

Fig. 254.   Cover the 20mm ($\frac{3}{4}$in) diameter section with linseed oil and brush a little inside the die. Using firm pressure push the work into the die and ensure the taper which is visible from the top of the die is just past the cutter. Maintaining pressure turn the *work* in a clockwise direction. When two or three threads are cut pressure can be relaxed, as the threaded part of the die will take up the drive, all that is necessary will be to continue to turn the work. Obviously it will be impossible to work the thread right up to the handle of the workpiece due to the guide plate on the die.

Fig. 255.   Remove the screw guide plate then carefully, so as not to dislodge or misalign the cutter as it now has no plate to protect it, replace the screw and complete the thread right up to the handle.

Fig. 256.   Replace the screw between centres, this time reversed with the handle at the tailstock end so that it will never be necessary to work towards the drive centre in the headstock. Work the handle to the desired design leaving just enough to be supported by the tailstock while it is polished before parting off with a chisel. Final finishing is done by hand as in Fig. 258 or the whole can be finished as described for Fig. 263–269.

Fig. 257. With the parting tool angled a little to the left, to produce a concave end to the screw, work in to leave about 3mm ($\frac{1}{8}$in) diameter which can be removed later on the bench with a knife, or with the long corner of the skew on the lathe.

Fig. 258. Where the die finishes it leaves a rather abrupt end to the thread, I use a 6mm ($\frac{1}{4}$in) gouge to work a cove at this point which adds to the appearance and removes the problem. Do not enter it as you would to work a normal cove as it would probably catch and run down the thread, spoiling it. Use it scraper-fashion pointed down as shown and take only the lightest of cuts. If you have a very narrow scraper so much the better.

Fig. 259. The style of the handle is limited only by your imagination. Most are straightforward between centre work, but one which is attractive, is shaped like a violin key. The photographs show several keys being made at the same time. Three pieces of prepared 25mm (1in) squared stuff are cramped together and marked out as in the photograph. These dimensions will produce screws approximately 20mm ($\frac{3}{4}$in) in diameter and 55mm (2$\frac{1}{4}$in) long. The outside pieces will be thrown away so only use waste pieces, they are merely to guide the drill.

Fig. 260 Use a sawtooth bit as this will require the minimum of hand-finishing. The centre dimension will vary with the size of the key required, but for a small one like this a 25mm (1in) bit was used off-set by a 3mm ($\frac{1}{8}$in) (fine) gauge line on the inside of the flanking pieces, thus leaving 6mm ($\frac{1}{4}$in) (fine) in the middle of the key. A really sharp sawtooth bit will leave a fine finish that can quickly be completed by hand.

Fig. 261. As the work will be part shaped be very careful in cross marking at both ends, tap in the drive centre and mount up to work in exactly the same way as Fig. 253. This key has a 12mm (½in) thread. Working the shank for threading towards the tailstock, complete the thread, and re-mount, reversed.

Fig. 262. Treat the handle as if it were a perfect cylinder and keep the lathe speed up to at least 2000 rpm as there is only a little timber to work. Don't be afraid of the tool catching when working this irregular shape, at this recommended speed or even slower it will not. You will see a slight blurr but with sharp tools, a gouge is best, it will hardly be felt. Finally part off with the long corner of a skew.

Fig. 263. On a small faceplate mount up a block of scrap approximately 75mm (3in) square by 100mm (4in) long, grain running as per the arrows. Threads cannot be worked effectively along the grain. With a 16mm (⅝in) diameter drill marked for depth work a hole about 75mm (3in) deep taking care not to go too deep or you will foul the faceplate. Keep the speed low, 350 rpm or less, any faster will overheat the auger, and high speeds will quickly dull a sawtooth bit and they are tedious to sharpen.

Fig. 264. Set the tap in the chuck held in the tailstock but do not switch on the lathe. Just hold the chuck stationary with the right hand and, after advancing the tailstock slightly to enter the tap into the hole, turn the headstock with the left hand towards you a quarter of a turn, advance the tailstock and repeat. Continue until at least one thread is complete, preferably a little more.

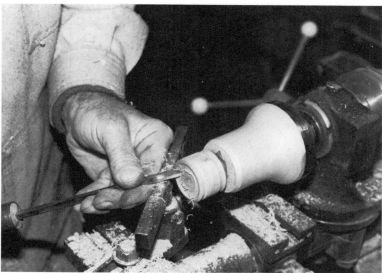

Fig. 265. Complete the rest of the thread by hand and finish with the bottoming tap. This is not absolutely necessary, but makes for a good accurate stop for the work that will be held in this jig.

The jig can, of course, be used indefinitely, and if this is the intention it would be best made from a hardwood, ideally beech. If it is removed from the faceplate be sure to mark it clearly to ensure it goes back in the same place, thus it will always be concentric.

Fig. 266. The jig is now ready to accept a part-finished piece of work that has only been threaded. The hold is positive, and as the jig was made and completed between centres, the work will run perfectly true. It is used for designs that call for a concave end, but, of course, any shape can be worked, sanded and polished in this mode with ease.

Fig. 267. A further aid is made from a length of threaded stuff which has a sawn slot in one end, to accept a screwdriver.

Fig. 268. This is screwed in to a pre-determined depth and the work screwed up tight against it to accommodate sanding, polishing or further work. It can also be used for final parting off, but do leave enough scrap protruding from the jig to remove the waste piece.

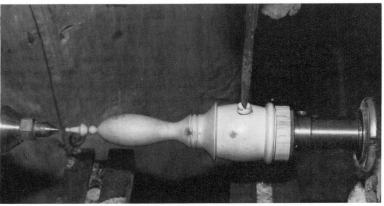

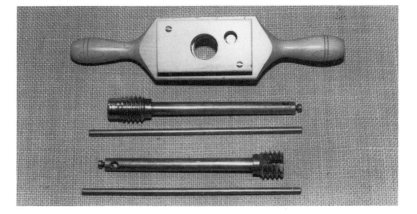

Fig. 269.   The finished piece jacked out ready for parting off. I am sure the method will suggest many other uses for those items that are tedious to finish between centres, whether the finished work needs to be threaded or not.

Fig. 270.   For a handled or goblet style nutcracker, a mandrel can be made up on a screw chuck. The cracker is made up and then reversed and mounted on the mandrel. If necessary a small bolt inserted in the threaded hole can be used to secure it. This should be covered with masking tape to prevent any likelihood of it being thrown out by vibration or centrifugal force.

Fig. 271.   In conclusion a word about thread boxes. To the best of my knowledge two types are available, both are well advertised one made in England the other in the U.S.A. For the following reasons I prefer the American.

The die has an aluminium threaded insert that offers eternal life to the tool, and the general quality is superior. The cutter is simplicity itself to adjust after honing, and has a very positive hold.

Not only are bottoming taps available, i.e. taps that will work a thread right to the base or a blind hole, they can be re-sharpened, are easy to enter, have the facility to eject swarf and do not need a tap wrench, as a tommy bar is supplied as standard.

An Arkansas stone to fit the cutters (one fits all three sizes) is offered as an extra, and will maintain the tool in tip-top condition, for fine work.

All that being said they are about a third more expensive than the U.K. make, and are only made in sizes of 12mm ($\frac{1}{2}$in), 19mm ($\frac{3}{4}$in) and 25mm (1in) at the time of writing.

Salt and pepper grinders

The task of neatly dividing between-centre turning so that it can be brought together again to match and fit, is not as difficult as it sounds. The techniques are discussed in this chapter and will have many applications.

To illustrate the principle I shall start with a conventional salt mill. The pepper mill is identical albeit the dimensions are slightly different. I had a length of Brazilian tulipwood, (*Dalbergia frutescens*) and my length would have given me a pair of 30cm (12in) mills but instead I decided to make a 30cm (12in) pepper mill, and a shorter salt and, if all went well, a mustard pot to show you how clever I am. One reference book on timber ends the section on tulipwood with the comment, 'seldom seen in the solid', thus as I had a little solid, I wanted to take no chances in wasting it due to a silly mistake.

Fig. 272.   As you will see in the picture, the two styles have been kept the same, but due to the difference in height, if any error had been made, it would have been possible to cover it up to some extent. The mustard pot is designed to complement the other two. Identical turnings are all very well, and indicate skill to some extent, but variations on a theme also have their place. In the second part we have the same thing only with a different type of mechanism, the handled style. The advantage of this mechanism is that there is no break for the capstan, which not only makes the work simpler but eliminates the inevitable miss-match of grain formation when the mill is used, and this is worth considering if using highly figured timber as in Fig. 300. Of the types available, they all are to all intents and purposes the same for fitting. The one we will discuss in part two is very neat and offers a stator fitting that is both easy to fit and is almost invisible and has a handle.

Fig. 273.   Three types of base fitting.

To cover the subject in as much detail as possible we will then look at the merits of the simple shaker, and due to the technique of completing in one mounting, very small, unusual or spectacular pieces of stuff can be used which otherwise might be scrap. Finally, the same item made in two sections with a rather professional method of manufacture that will be found to be much more convenient to fill using a method which has many other applications.

Fig. 274. With the stuff mounted between centres work to a cylinder. The parting cut to facilitate mounting in the 6-in-1 chuck is prepared, with either a parting tool or a 10mm (⅜in) beading and parting tool which is the ideal size for the work. From the headstock end of the work mark in a 10mm (⅜in) wide, 45mm (1¾in) diameter, rebate. The two halves of the chuck rings *must* meet and be a snug fit for the best results. They use a dovetail action to draw the stuff against the chuck body by applying the pressure to the cramping ring.

With the work set up in the chuck, drill the required size hole or a preliminary, smaller diameter hole in the end as far as required or as far as the length of the drill used will permit. Two light cuts are always preferred to one grindingly hefty one so the smaller diameter hole can be enlarged by a larger drill to the desired diameter.

Fig. 275. Measure the retaining bar as this is the first part to be fitted. I prefer to use a vernier for this work but calipers can be used. I like to set this into a worked rebate, rather than go to the trouble of producing two housings which is sometimes unsightly. Bring the tool rest to a position across the area to be worked, and set at a height that will permit the point of a skew chisel to enter on the centre line.

Fig. 276. If you have a selection of sawtooth bits, one may be of a size to accommodate the bar, if not, use the size nearest and enlarge to the required diameter with a skew. At this point the height of the mill can, to some extent, be varied. If when working with a 100mm (4in) mechanism the stator is inserted 25mm (1in) in, the overall height will be increased to a finished size of approximately 125mm (5in). Mechanisms are available up to 460mm (18in) long and if a longer one is required, the bar can be cut in half and an insert welded or brazed in to achieve the required length, as in Fig. 332–333. If it is intended to fit the stator in to some depth, mark the drill with tape.

Fig. 277. In the absence of sawtooth bits the work can be completed quickly and accurately with a skew. Take only light cuts, use only the point of the tool and keep it sharp. Present it to the work in the horizontal and in line with the lathe bed.

Fig. 278.   The retaining bar fitted, snugly. Note the spelch in the bore hole which will be removed when we come to fit the stator.

Fig. 279.   Set a vernier to the size of the stator as was done for the retaining bar, work the necessary fitting for the stator, and with a very light cut remove the ensuing spelch. Take care not to disturb the size of the bore hole, if you do it will not fit the mandrel which can be either a homemade one or the patent variety.

Fig. 280.   With the stator and retaining bar fitted, the rebate for the stator flange wants to be exactly the depth of the thickness of the large diameter ring, or flange of the stator. If you do go in too far, the error can easily be remedied by working the rebate for the retaining bar in a little further, but beware of spelch as you will be working up to a net rebate. It will be appreciated that the aforementioned is reciprocal, but there is a limit.

Fig. 281.   Most verniers are fitted with a depth gauge, use this to establish the depth of the large diameter flange next to my right hand forefinger, assemble the mechanism with the top nut screwed on to its limit and mark the overall length. Remember to add to this dimension the amount that will be removed in cutting off the capstan head and forming the upstand of approximately 6mm ($\frac{1}{4}$in).

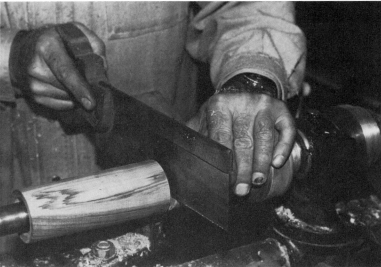

Fig. 282.   Using a parting tool cut in to a depth of 12mm ($\frac{1}{2}$in) or so to mark the length of the mill. The tailstock with a revolving centre, or with a plug and a dead centre, can be used to support the work.

Fig. 283.   To conserve valuable and rare timber and to avoid mismatching the grain as much as is possible, the capstan should be parted off with as little waste as possible. For instance, if you use a 10mm ($\frac{3}{8}$in) parting tool, the waste will be approximately 20mm ($\frac{3}{4}$in) and unacceptable. So use a narrow parting tool and, assuming the bore hole is a diameter of 25mm (1in), set a vernier to a diameter of 32mm (1$\frac{1}{4}$in) and make the first parting cut to this dimension. This cut will produce the upstand or flange on which the capstan will revolve.

Fig. 284.   With the same or a narrower parting tool, make a further cut on the headstock side of the capstan almost, but not completely parting off. This will leave a smooth finish to the top of the upstand and the inside of the capstan and although this part will not be visible in use it will be seen when the mill is filled with pepper corns or rock salt, so it might as well be tidy.

Fig. 285.   The body can now be parted off with a fine tenon saw held up to the capstan; take care not to damage the upstand or the inside of the capstan. There will be no fear of anything jamming and marking or damaging the work, not to mention the fact that it will completely spoil the precision if the stuff left in the chuck is disturbed. Mills made in this sequence must run dead true, as the entire work of fitting the mechanism and working the capstan fitting is completed in one mounting and entirely from one direction.

Fig. 286.   The body of the mill felled off showing the upstand. Notice that there is a clear mark on the face of the capstan that can be used as a guide. To avoid spelch, drill to a depth of just a fraction more than the height of the upstand. The upstand in the body is fitted into the capstan to a tight fit, the tighter the better, it can be eased later to run sweetly.

Fig. 287.   Fortuitously the drive discs I use are exactly 19mm ($\frac{3}{4}$in) diameter so a sawtooth bit of this size is used to set them. The work can, of course, be completed with a skew as for the stator. I like to set them in about 12mm ($\frac{1}{2}$in) so they are there but not seen.

Fig. 288.   The drive disc fitted into the capstan, and the rebate to accept the upstand on the mill body completed. It makes for a better finish if the screw holes in the drive disc are countersunk, and countersunk screws are used to secure it. Keeping the slots of the screws matching, i.e. in the same direction tends to make them less visible. Carefully sand and finish the end grain.

Fig. 289.   Satisfied that the drive disc is fitted snug the final drilling for the shaft of the mill mechanism can be completed. With most mechanisms a 6mm ($\frac{1}{4}$in) drill will be required. If only a mill is being made, a hole can be drilled right through. The 6-in-1 is hollow on the inside so no damage will be done if the drill goes too far and you will feel it break through. If, as here, it is intended to make a mustard pot, napkin ring, etc., in the same mounting, the drill should be marked for depth with tape.

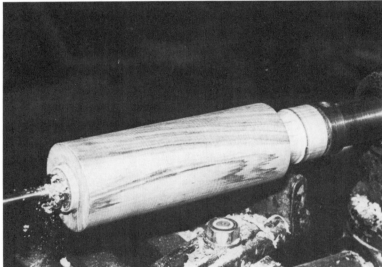

Fig. 290. The fitting for the mechanism is now complete, and all from one direction. The picture shows the tight fit recommended between the body and the capstan. It is now only necessary to part off the capstan.

Fig. 291. The capstan parted off; note the hole completely through the capstan with just the tip of the drill marking the waste part of the next project, in this case a mustard pot. The 6-in-1 chuck can now be set aside and the mill completed.

Fig. 292. Mount up a piece of waste stuff on a screw chuck; you can do it between centres but a screw chuck is more convenient. Work it to a very snug fit, *not* tapered, to the bore hole in the body of the mill. Slip the mill body on to this mandrel with the stator fitting to the headstock. If your mandrel is well made this will permit the work to run as true as in its original mounting. Details for making a mandrel are shown on page 97.

Fig. 293. The other end, the part that the original drilling could not reach, can now be completed. This will, of course, apply to mills of 150mm (6in) or more in height, for shorter mills take care not to bore the 25mm (1in) diameter hole too far in the original working, as this will pass into the capstan and might make the fitting of the drive disc difficult. Finish the drilling.

Fig. 294.   With this final boring completed. If this is very slightly out of true, as can sometimes happen when work is reversed, it will make no difference to the true running of the mill when grinding pepper, or the turning of the capstan. If you wish to sand the end grain, you can either do so now or when the shaping work is completed.

Fig. 295.   To complete the mill place the capstan in its snug fitting on the body of the mill, bring up the tailstock to support it, and work to the desired design. Beware! It is easy to forget, in your enthusiasm, that as the work has a 25mm (1in) hole through most of it no part should be less than 30mm (1¼in) diameter. Sand and polish, and before removing the body from the mandrel, a light touch with fine abrasive on the upstand, testing constantly, will render the turn of the capstan firm and positive, and this can be further improved with the application of a little wax furniture polish.

Fig. 296.   The original chuck still containing the mustard pot can now be returned to the lathe. With a few gossamer light cuts from a gouge, work the lid top to a finish and sand and polish. Use the same method as for the capstan head of the mill to produce a small upstand in the lid, just enough to locate inside the pot. The diameter of the upstand will of course be the same diameter as that of the glass insert that will be fitted. Then part off the finished lid.

Fig. 297.   With a drill or skew, or combination of both, work the recess to fit the small glass insert which should fit just below the level of the top of the pot to allow the lid rebate (upstand) to sit in. Make sure the insert is a slack, but not sloppy fit as it will be removed for washing. Sand and polish the inside.

Fig. 298. Any final adjustments to the fitting of the lid must be made before the work is removed from the chuck. When you are satisfied that the inside is neat and tidy, make a light indent with a pointed awl in the centre of the base inside, this will facilitate the locating of the tailstock for the next operation.

Fig. 299. Remove the work from the chuck and mount between centres. The drive in its original setting is supported by the tailstock located in the prepared indent. The outside can now be completed, sanded and polished. The only part of the exercise that cannot be finished on the lathe is the inside of the box lid. If this is parted off with a very sharp tool, however, it will be but a simple matter to sand by hand, seal and polish.

Fig. 300 The finished handled set in Pau Rosa. This method will demonstrate one way of getting the most out of the available material. It also illustrates one way of making a small box.

Fig. 301. With the stuff turned to a cylinder and a dowel of such dimensions as will fit the collet used, in this case approximately 20mm ($\frac{3}{4}$in) diameter produced, we can look at the merits of the Coronet chuck. It is a form of engineers' chuck, with the three jaws closing on the prepared dowel as the ring is tightened. The tools are supplied with the chuck.

Fig. 302. Support the work in the chuck and commence drilling. Again I would emphasise that using progressively larger drills will produce a better job than one hefty cut, it will also lengthen the life of the cutting edges of the tools. These comments do not apply to machine augers. An inside diameter of approximately 19mm ($\frac{7}{8}$in) will be required, although the mechanisms do vary.

Fig. 303. The drilling of the main body of the mill completed, either the top can be fitted as here or the mechanism for the base can be installed, as described in Fig. 276–280. If you mount up a blank a little longer than required, any error in the fitting of either end and it will be a simple matter to part it off and start again. This will, of course, apply to many projects that require ironmongery to be fitted.

Fig. 304.   You will need to reverse the work, possibly for further drilling and certainly to complete the other end fitting. For this a mandrel can be made up as in Fig. 312 or, as here, using a further attachment to the Coronet chuck. Various sizes are available and, incidentally, a similar attachment is also available for the 6-in-1 chuck. Note that the spindle has a tapered groove machined, tapered towards the periphery of the spindle, a pin is supplied and when this pin is sited in the deepest part of the taper it is level with the diameter of the spindle and will permit work to be pushed on unhindered, when such work is then twisted, by starting the lathe or by holding the chuck still and revolving the work away from you, the pin rises in the taper and locks the work on the spindle.

Fig. 305.   A close-up of the pin chuck. Take care not to drop the pin, it is very small and difficult to find in the shavings under the lathe. Also note that the spindle is not only hollow, but tapered.

Fig. 306.   The work mounted as above. The positive lock enables the work of the fitting of the stator and further drilling to be completed.

Fig. 307.   A close-up of the stator used for this type of mechanism, note that it is without a flange and makes a very neat fitting. The sides of the stator are splined and are a push fit in a shouldered hole 24mm ($\frac{15}{16}$in) diameter and 10mm ($\frac{5}{8}$in) deep. The second, larger diameter hole is not necessary but I feel makes for neatness. Full instructions in way of dimensions come with the mechanisms, but other than the recommended sizes for the top and the stator, which must, of course, be adhered to, other dimensions can, to some extent, vary to suit your design ideas.

Fig. 308.   If you have made one of the pair freehand this can be used to lay off the main parts of the 'mate' and the turning completed by eye, making full use of calipers or vernier. Note the extra length mentioned which would, of course, be removed if not required before the final work of fitting is completed. The alternative to completing by eye would be either to make your own template or, as in Fig. 317, use one of the profile gauges available.

Fig. 309.   To work the desired style, a plug to fit the tailstock end is worked, inserted, and the tailstock is brought up to support. It then becomes straightforward between centres turning.

   For this pepper mill and salt shaker I have used an Amazonian timber, Pau Rosa which is from the tulipwood family, *Zygrophylacea*.

Salt, pepper and sugar shakers

Fig. 310.   Salt, pepper and sugar shakers. From left to right, Israeli olive; English wild pear; Chin-Chang. The funnel for filling the containers is English plane or lacewood. It is made by adapting the goblet technique described on page 104.

Fig. 311.   To reduce waste the blank must be accurately cross marked and set up in some form of jig. I am using a small engineers' vice, but a simple jig held with G cramps will do just as well. The main hole is drilled to within 12mm ($\frac{1}{2}$in) of the top of the shaker according to the design. The diameter will be governed by the size of the bung used so that it fits snugly. To accommodate the flange of the bung and to facilitate its easy removal, a second, larger diameter hole about 10mm ($\frac{3}{8}$in) deep will be worked next while still in the jig to ensure it is centred.

If using auger type drills it is best to drill the large diameter first, with sawtooth drills either way is possible. For any drill select the slowest speed possible for a clean, straight hole, and avoid excessive pressure. An alternative method would be to mount the blank in the lathe set up in a screw chuck, but this would produce more waste.

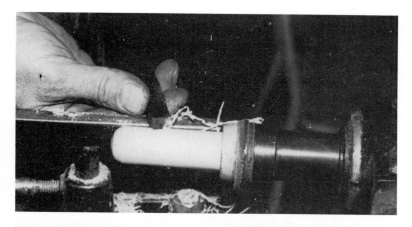

Fig. 312. To make the mandrel mount a piece of scrap of the required size in a screw chuck. If you are making several shakers at the same time use a hardwood. It is best if the mandrel is long enough to pass the half-way mark of the work it is to hold by 12mm ($\frac{1}{2}$in) or so. Rough turn to within a little of the finished size and finish carefully to a snug fit for the blank to be eased on, preferably with a chisel. Do *not* taper the mandrel, it must be parallel. If the fit is really snug and it is difficult to get the blank to slide on, don't take another cut as this may make it too slack. Just a touch with fine 350 grit abrasive paper while the lathe is still running, followed by a wax candle and repeated as necessary will obtain a good snug fit. The effort will be worth it as this mandrel can be used many times, for all sorts of jobs.

Fig. 313. With the internal work complete, the blank can be slipped on to the prepared mandrel and worked to a cylinder, supported by the tailstock.

Fig. 314. Before too much of the design detail is worked on the body, it is best to complete the top. Here I am producing a slight taper to the top with a chisel. The same principles apply here as when working a cove with a gouge. On entering the tool it must be completely on its side and at right-angles to the work; if not it will skid in the direction in which it is angled. Take only fine cuts to render a surface that will require little sanding to finish. Take care not to foul the steel centre.

Fig. 315. With the top completed the design detail of the body can be completed. Worked in this sequence, if a slip when working the top does occur the damage can be eradicated now.

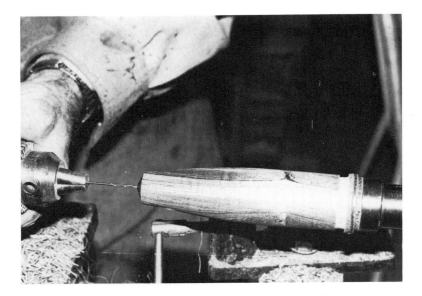

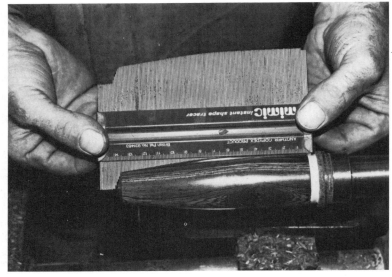

Fig. 316. All work completed, the tailstock can be fitted with an engineers' chuck (Jacobs chuck) and a fine drill, not much larger than 2mm ($\frac{1}{16}$in). Whilst I have used a revolving centre a dead centre could also be used and, if so, leave the drilling and the top detail to the last operation, thus if any staining or burning occasioned by the dead centre occurs, drilling and one very careful cut will have the effect of tidying up. For obvious reasons a revolving centre is a great asset.

Fig. 317. Sand and polish, and if making more than one use the original to prepare a template for subsequent identical turnings.

The timber used for these two shakers is Chin-Chang, or Siamese (Thai) rosewood.

Shakers with screw tops

Fig. 318. Set up a timber suitable for threading in the screw chuck. Box, beech and fruitwoods are ideal, or the same timber as the shaker could be used. We will be using the 20mm ($\frac{3}{4}$in) thread, so work to a 20mm ($\frac{3}{4}$in) diameter and, while still in the lathe, two or three turns will produce the thread. With a suitable drill produce a hole to a depth of twice the thread length, 10mm ($\frac{3}{8}$in) in diameter.

Fig. 319. Take a parting tool and work a shank 10mm ($\frac{3}{8}$in) long to a diameter of 14mm ($\frac{9}{16}$in) and with the tool offered up to the work on its side, cut a few fine rings as these will help the adhesive to grip. With the long corner of a skew held on its side part off.

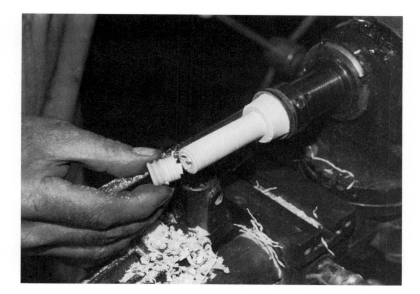

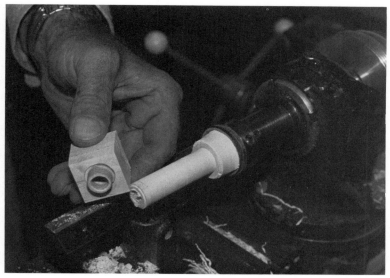

Fig. 320.   Such plugs have many uses so while the sized stuff is in the lathe, it will be a good time to make a few more to keep for use at a later date. Try not to handle the shank as natural or mineral oils will impede adhesion.

Fig. 321.   Most timbers will not satisfactorily accept a tap along the grain, i.e. into end grain. Therefore, take a length of close-grained timber such as beech, fruitwood holly or box prepared true to the following dimensions, 32mm × 25mm × 152mm ($1\frac{1}{4}$in × 1in × 6in) the longer it is, the easier to handle. At regular intervals drill 16mm ($\frac{5}{8}$in) holes, complete the 20mm ($\frac{3}{4}$in) threads and separate the threaded sections equally. This will give what will in effect be the 'nut' as I call it. Set this assembly aside.

Fig. 322.   Set up the stuff with which the shaker is to be made in a screw chuck, with due allowance for parting off when completed. At the tailstock end work a dowel that will fit one of the collet chucks. This dowel will be used in the finished product so the collet nearest to the size of the finished product, should be selected to reduce waste. The work could be drilled, and, when reversed, mounted on a screw chuck, but this would involve more waste.

Fig. 323.   With the required dowel, or spigot worked, and the stuff turned to a rough cylinder, if necessary make a location mark. I have done this in this piece but the split in the stuff would have sufficed. With your thinnest parting tool work a parting cut to a depth that will be convenient to separate with a fine tenon saw, as we did in Fig. 285.

Fig. 324.   With the top separated, the body can be prepared and hollowed out to a diameter, or series of diameters, that will accommodate the design. I would mention that other than the working of the stuff for actual threading, other dimensions are not critical and can be varied to some extent if drills are not available to the size suggested. I have commenced with a 25mm (1in) diameter sawtooth to a depth of 12mm ($\frac{1}{2}$in). Further boring with decreasing diameter drills say 3mm ($\frac{1}{8}$in) at a time, will suit tapered styles. The first 12mm ($\frac{1}{2}$in) drilling, shouldered by subsequent smaller drilling, will accommodate the nut when turned.

Fig. 325.   The top can now be set up in the collet chuck and worked either by drilling, or by a combination of drilling and finishing to size with the long corner of a skew chisel, in the same way as when fitting stators in grinders. Enough must be worked to accept the threaded plug, or

'bolt' as it has become. The remainder of the top end can be 'stepped' as required to accommodate the design, see Fig. 337.

Fig. 326.   The bolt is glued in the top with a suitable adhesive, and allowed to set.

Fig. 327.   With the adhesive set to allow light handling, and with the top still in the collet chuck, screw on the nut, bring up the tailstock to support and work the nut to a cylinder of 25mm (1in) diameter. Now reduce with a parting tool its length to 12mm ($\frac{1}{2}$in). This will provide a spigot to be inserted in the top of the body of the shaker.

Fig. 328.   Re-mount the body, which will still be set up in the screw chuck, in the lathe and line up the locating marks. Fix the top with nut and bolt assembled into the body with adhesive using the lathe as a cramp. Take care not to allow any adhesive squeeze to escape and lock the top to the body. One way to avoid this would be to carefully apply wax to the parts that *do not* require to be glued, avoiding any contamination with the parts that *do*. Allow the adhesive to set before proceeding with the turning.

Fig. 329.   The shaker can now be worked to the desired design, and a fine hole drilled to complete the work, all treated as if it were one solid piece. Made this way it can be unscrewed for filling, and always screws up again, with the grain in a perfect match as shown in Fig. 310.

The joint can be worked at the lower part of the shaker if the particular style required makes this more convenient but bear in mind that it will not be quite so convenient to fill. It is also worth mentioning, that salt particularly and sugar are moisture absorbent and even very dry timber will retain some moisture content. After a few days the first filling will probably become solid, having drawn all or most of the moisture out of the timber. Poke this out, but don't throw it away, kept in a tin in a warm place to dry out it can be re-used for the same purpose. The second filling will, in most instances, be unaffected. This method is preferable to placing the shaker on or near some source of heat, such as a radiator. The timber won't like it, reacting by splitting or warping. Gentle acclimatization of timber is always to be preferred.

Fig. 330 and 331.   Sugar shaker showing detail of nut and bolt and match of grain when assembled.

Fig. 332. While mechanisms come in a wide range of lengths, sometimes, due to a particular style, or to get the best from a very special piece of timber, it is necessary to lengthen or shorten the shaft. The following method is simple. Cut the shaft in half and insert a length of similar diameter steel taken from the shank of a bolt or similar. Place this assembly in a piece of angle iron held in a metalwork vice and braze the two joints. In the example I have used an arc weld, but silver solder using an ordinary gas blow lamp with a fine nozzle is just as strong and neater.

Fig. 333. The joints can then be ground to tidy the work and if the heat generated has distorted the shaft, gentle tapping with the ball peen of a light hammer using the shape of the angle iron as a template will quickly straighten the shaft. This can be checked by revolving it in the template.

Goblets and scoops

Fig. 334.   From left to right in the background: English walnut (*Juglans regia*); English Yew (*Taxus baccata*); Cocobolo (*Dalbergia retusa*); Hornbeam (*Carpinus betulus*); Sassafrass (*Atherosperma moschatum*); Olive (*Olie*).
   In the foreground: English Yew (*Taxus baccata*); Hornbeam (*Carpinus betulus*); Chestnut (*Castanea*).

The technique for working goblets uses the method to produce scoops for use in the kitchen.

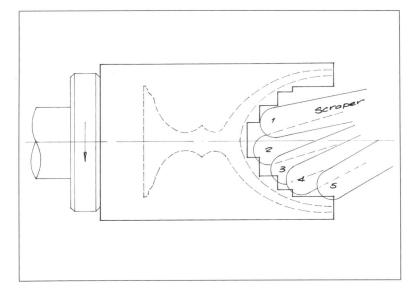

Fig. 335.   Using a piece of hornbeam will give me the opportunity to expand on the use of scrapers as a necessary tool for the turner. I will for the sake of clarity call this project a goblet until I change it into a scoop, then look at the method of finishing a goblet with a different style. I am also doing this goblet the hard way, inasmuch the outside is *net* sized as it is a small log and thus the inside must be worked to it. Of course, it is not only much more convenient to do it the other way round, it is the correct way.

Starting with a small diameter drill, progressively enlarge the inside to a pre-determined depth marked by taping the drill shank. Take great care to stick to the marks, an extra twist on the tailstock handle with the final drill of large diameter will pull the workpiece off the chuck.

Fig. 336.   As I do not have a drill of convenient size to complete the removal of the waste by drilling, a skew chisel with a sharp point is used to work to the desired thickness.

Fig. 337.   The inside, which cannot photograph successfully is shown in the drawing which represents the inside shape that would be produced with a succession of drills increasing in size followed by cuts with the scraper.

Fig. 338.   Use calipers to ensure the walls are of a constant thickness.

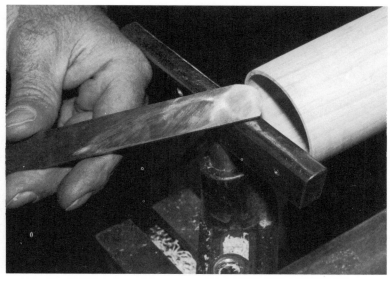

Fig. 339.   The skew chisel used in this way, will, on some timbers, leave a ragged effect and added to this, it is not easy to see what you are doing in such a confined shape. A gouge is difficult or even impossible to use for some shapes, therefore a scraper is the only alternative, and it is used as much by feel as anything. As in the drawing, it is presented to the work contacting to the right of centre, where the stuff is revolving *upwards* so that no cutting can commence. Then, with the contact felt, draw the scraper to the left slowly and gently, taking the lightest of cuts, there will be little waste to remove so don't try to rush it.

Fig. 340.   The shape of the scraper used will depend on the profile of the intended design. Just to make it as difficult as possible I have chosen a near flat base for this one. The scraper shape used is what one might call a semi half-round, well rounded to the left and the right side also rounded slightly to prevent any tendency for a point to

mark the work as the tool is pulled round the curve of the base.

Fig. 341.   Hold the tool gently but firmly, always slightly inclined downwards and using the tool-rest fingers as a pivot point, stroke the work gently. Keep the scraper very sharp at all times.

Fig. 342.   The work of the scraper completed, the inside must now be sanded and polished. This must be done at this stage as any sideways pressure later, especially when the stem is worked could snap the workpiece at its weakest point.

Fig. 343. Bridge the top of the goblet with a thin rule and establish the *exact* depth of the inside. The vernier is the best tool for this as its depth prong will calibrate with the jaws, and precise measurements can be established. Failure to do this might result in you suddenly finding a ring drops into your hand!

Fig. 344. Transfer the depth measurement to the outside of the goblet with a clear heavy mark. This will be the base of the inside and if worked up to will produce the ring, which is not what we want!

Fig. 345. Working well into the waste, using a parting tool, the shaping of the outside of the goblet can be started. To enable the calipers or fingers to get at the work to judge thickness, some form of V cut must be made to remove the waste. Work in a little with the parting tool.

Fig. 346. Keeping well away from the pencil mark, open up the parting tool cut with a gouge, working from both sides to form a V and start to work the shape of the goblet.

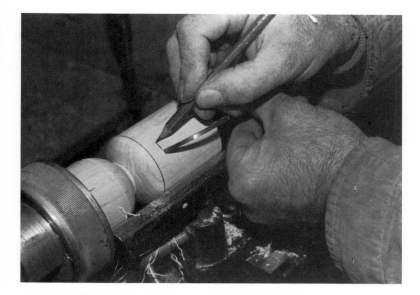

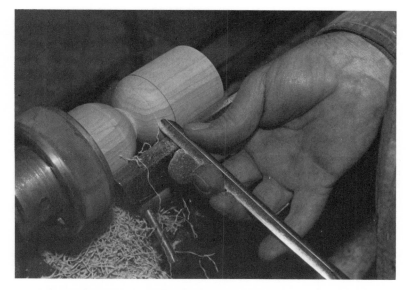

Fig. 347. Using the calipers set to the thickness of the wall of the goblet, slide them down to the point where the base starts to curve. Make a further mark at this point and pencil in heavily.

Fig. 348. Using your fingers, sometimes more reliable than calipers, test for thickness, you will now be able to override the original mark as this was for the extreme depth.

Fig. 349. Take your time, this is an exciting experience. Make sure the tool is sharp so no heavy pressure will be required and take light cuts. Take care to keep a constant check on the thickness with your fingers, you will soon acquire the 'feel'. You can, with care, use your fingers with the lathe running but beware of burns. If you wish to use calipers or vernier you *must* switch off, or the inside will be scarred.

Fig. 350. Continue to shape the goblet and at the same time reduce some of the waste from the chuck end as well.

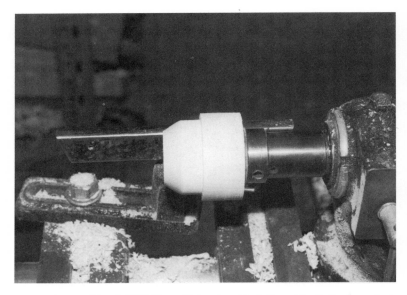

Fig. 351.   Your fingers will tell you when enough is enough. Don't be tempted to try 'just one more cut', not to start with anyway. Now is the time to establish a stopping point, that is a point that will produce some form of edge up to which the bowl of the goblet can be sanded and polished and won't be interfered with when the stem is commenced.

Fig. 352.   Sand and polish the bowl to a complete finish up as far as the pencil mark. This is where we depart from the goblet and turn it into a shovel, scoop, or trowel. We will pick up the goblet work from this point later on in Fig. 365.

Fig. 353.   Using the softest timber you have, set it up in a screw chuck. Work a mandrel that will be a snug fit to the inside of the goblet; not so tight that it will mark the polish but not sloppy either. Start by sizing the outer end of the mandrel, about 3mm ($\frac{1}{8}$in) of its length, then if this is too slack the next 3mm ($\frac{1}{8}$in) can be a little less, finally taper the end slightly to help minimise damage to the polished interior.

Fig. 354.   As the work was begun in the 6-in-1 and was originally mounted between centres to effect the fitting for this chuck, it will still have a clear centre marking. Even if the fit to the mandrel is perfect, you can still place one thickness of tissue paper round the mandrel prior to pushing the workpiece on to protect it, then the tailstock is used to support for final turning.

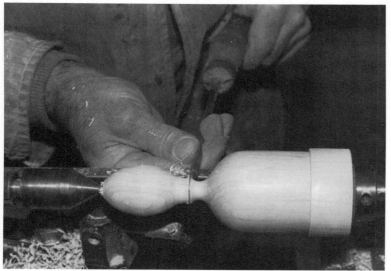

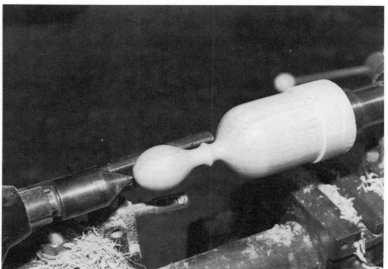

Fig. 355.   The worst of the waste is removed, and the shaping of the scoop handle can commence. A roughing-out gouge or spindle gouge can be used to form the rough shape or to make an enlarged version of a style you have in mind. If you do not like it, there will be plenty of stuff left to re-style it.

Fig. 356.   Use a spindle gouge for the finishing touches, with the rest high enough to permit the gouge to be presented with the handle five degrees or so below the horizontal. Work carefully up to the pencil finishing mark.

Fig. 357.   If you are really confident with the chisel, a skew is the tool to effect a fine finish, and it is a lovely cut to make round a convex surface like this. Do not separate completely at this time, but work the finish as far as possible, leaving just the smallest pip as support. Sand and polish with the work supported. Finally, with a skew presented long corner down use it to sever the pip.

Fig. 358.   The handle completed. Any sanding or polishing required at the tailstock end can be effected now as the pressure required will be on the extreme end and so it will not disturb the work on the mandrel. For obvious reasons do not attempt any further polishing on any other part as this will push the work off the mandrel.

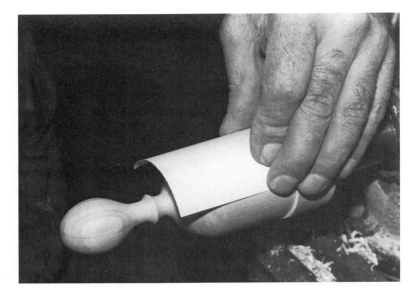

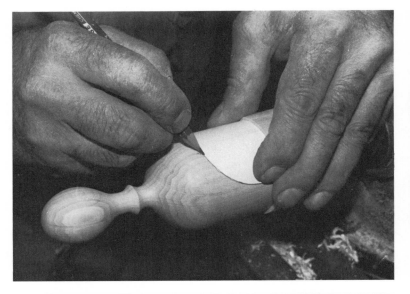

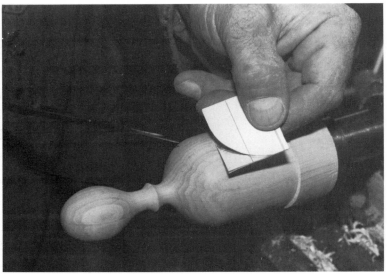

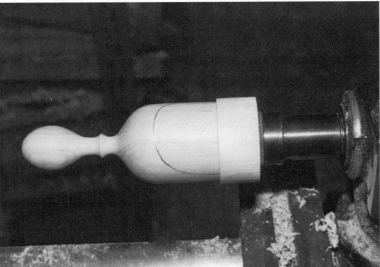

Fig. 359.   With the workpiece still on the mandrel, which makes it easy to handle, take a piece of paper and cut to length.

Fig. 360.   Fold in half and either freehand or with compasses mark and cut to shape.

Fig. 361.   Using the stop of the mandrel to line up the paper pattern, lay it on and mark out the cutting line.

Fig. 362.   By using the pusher (Fig. 214) to hold the work in place the profile can be removed with a fine coping saw, cutting into the mandrel if necessary, or if only making one of a size. I cut mine out with the bandsaw, but the coarseness of the skiptooth blades requires a little more hand sanding. If you are lucky enough to have a belt sander use it for finishing, and for a little more shaping if required.

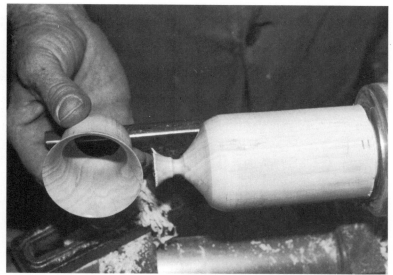

Fig. 363.   The finished scoop.

Fig. 364.   An excellent indication of what not to do, I
would like to tell you that this was prepared deliberately for
the purpose of demonstration, it wasn't, it happened when
turning too thin without constant reference to the calipers.
It is presented as an indication of either carelessness, over
confidence, or inattention to detail, or better still a mixture
of all. When this sort of thing happens at demonstrations I
have to think quickly and say, with nonchalance, 'now all
you have to do is work a handle and fit it and you have a
bell', I doubt it really ever fools anyone!

Fig. 365.   Returning to the goblet, this time with a
different design work the bowl to the desired size and
shape. Take time to check constantly with the calipers and
when finished polish inside and out right up to the cove
indicated with the pencil. The area thus polished must *not*
be touched again as this design has a long delicate stem, so
inspect carefully until entirely satisfied with the finish.

Fig. 366.   Quite a lot of waste must now be removed, and
while I am working here with a spindle gouge a roughing-
out gouge could also be used. As you approach the final
working of the stem very fine and gentle cuts will be
required, so if this is the first time you have tackled this
type of work you will have plenty of time and stuff to
practise the light touch.

Fig. 367. Make a cut with the parting tool to establish the length of the goblet, not too deep at this stage and do not work the diameter of the base to its final size. Then, if a slip occurs as the base is worked, there will be plenty of stuff left to make good the error. Continue working the stem with cuts from left to right, gradually bringing the bowl end to the desired diameter at a point approximately in the middle of the stem.

Fig. 368. Working from right to left and taking only the lightest of cuts complete the first 25mm (1in) or so of the bowl end of the stem. If the timber used is suspect – a little soft or brittle – this part can be sanded and polished, perhaps as far as indicated by the arrow in Fig. 371.

Fig. 369. With the gouge completely on its side, in the same way as a cove would be started, the final cuts can be made. It is at this point that a slip which scars the base is most likely, but if the size has been left full it will be easy to remove later.

Fig. 370. The gouge is rolled down the base and, following the shape and with the lightest pressure on the tool, work along the stem to the point of the last polishing. If this leaves a slight joining mark don't worry about it, remember the part that is polished will be a different colour, or shade, and the join will be invisible after sanding. Alternatively, a detail of design could be worked as in the cocobolo goblet in the group on page 103, which gives a stop/start point. Do not be tempted to work all the way up to the base of the bowl until you have made one or two goblets.

Fig. 371. Shown in close-up, the fine finishing cut that will be continued up to the arrowed point. To stop, the tool handle is lowered rather than removed, thus bringing the cutting edge off the work.

Fig. 372. The thickness of the base can now be established using the parting tool. Take it into the waste to leave enough material to support the work for final sanding and polishing.

Fig. 373. The whole stem can now be sanded and polished. If necessary support the stem with light pressure from a finger above. When sanding always try to support one hand with the other as shown. Take extra care when working at the bowl end of the stem. If the stem is fine any undue pressure on the work will set up an oscillation which could fracture it.

Fig. 374. Alternatively, hold the abrasive paper over the stem. I prefer this method as it avoids any pressure from the fingers, and is a more controlled approach. In most hardwoods, if the work has been completed using newly-honed tools for the final cuts, little more than 220 grit garnet, or similar, will be required moving to 350 or a little finer, and finishing with steel wool. Take care to make a tidy pad of steel wool without any strands hanging loose for they will wrap round the work and snatch the pad from your hands, possibly snapping the stem in the process.

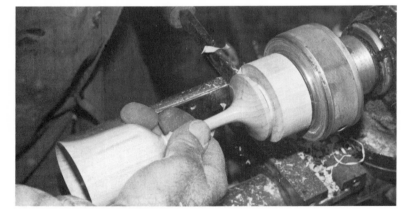

Fig. 375. Finally polish with friction polish. A second pad held on top will give the little extra pressure necessary for this type of finish. Watch for the loose ends or threads of cloth, for the same reasons as steel wool.

Fig. 376. It is the most natural thing in the world to let the polishing cloth run up the stem and round the bowl – I have stopped the lathe for the illustration. Resist it, it will almost certainly snap the stem if you do!

Fig. 377. Any practise in holding a vernier or calipers with one hand, and the parting tool in the other will stand you in good stead for parting off. This is another simple

and straight-forward operation, but like everything else, is an acquired skill. If in doubt, work down to a dowel of approximately 6mm ($\frac{1}{4}$in) diameter and separate with a tenon saw.

Fig. 378. If parted with the tool the pip can be removed on the bench with a knife or chisel, and the piece is ready for a felt base. Or, as we did with the scoop, a mandrel can be prepared and with the work on the mandrel supported either by a revolving centre or the pusher, the base can be sanded and polished. Start at the edge and work towards the apex of the base, not the other way round. The final finishing with the supporting centre removed takes place with all the pressure of the sanding/polishing being applied in line with the workpiece to avoid it moving on the mandrel and damaging the polish on the inside.

Fig. 379. Note the difference in colour, both pieces are in hornbeam, the goblet finished with clear friction polish, the scoop with a twenty-four hour soak in Danish oil.

Boxes

Returning to the use of timber in its natural form I thought it would be an opportunity to study the use of logs. This practice can result in disappointment if you are not using sound dry stuff, as timber in this form will be subject to considerable movement after working. If you have a store of logs that have dried without checking there is no reason to expect them to do anything exciting after working, and the grain effects that can be obtained using this method will be most unusual as well as economically preserving precious and dwindling resources.

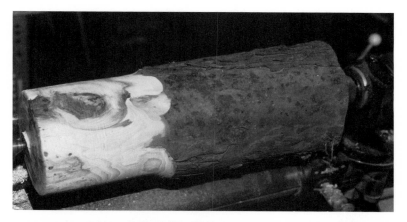

Fig. 380.   I weighed a yew log at intervals of one month over a period of two years and for two months the weight had stablilised. I felt it was dry enough to use and I elected to complete the turning in one operation, and it was a complete success. If there is still any doubt as to the stability of the stuff, rough work all the following stages and set the pieces aside for a few weeks. The whole can then be finally worked, finished and polished as in Fig. 389–390.

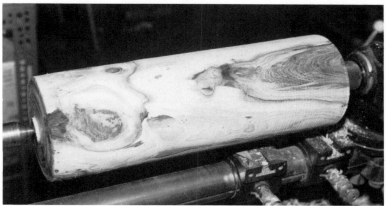

Fig. 381.   The log roughed down, I decided the headstock end would be ideal for the box I had in mind. A fitting for the split ring fixing for the 6-in-1 was worked at the headstock end, and the required length for the intended box was separated with a parting tool. The remainder was set aside for other uses, one of which is the champagne glass shown in Fig. 334.

Fig. 382.   Set up in the 6-in-1, the necessary reduction of stuff to allow the clamping ring clearance will form the base so thus far no waste at all. The outer end will become the top half, or lid of the box. Turn to shape using a hemisphere template. Allowance must be made both for the double rebate which will be required to fit the lid, 3mm ($\frac{1}{8}$in) each is ample for both lid and base, and a further 3mm ($\frac{1}{8}$in) allowance for parting off, making 9mm ($\frac{3}{8}$in) in all.

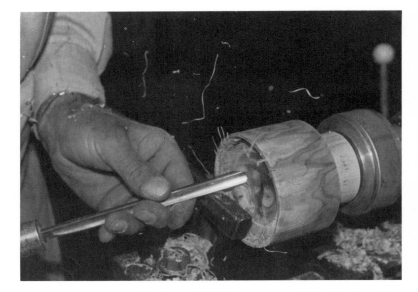

Fig. 383.   With the top rebate worked, and a 20mm (¾in) rebate to accept the mini-collet, the whole of the top of the box can be sanded and polished.

Fig. 384.   A parting tool is used to separate the two halves leaving a small dowel to be cut through with a fine tenon saw. As the top is polished it would be a shame to drop it which might happen if it was parted off completely with the parting tool. The top is set aside safely.

Fig. 385.   With the base still in the 6-in-1 chuck the inside can be completed. I use a 10mm (⅜in) spindle gouge to remove the worst of the waste, finishing off with a 6mm (¼in) and, if necessary, a scraper for final finishing. The inside rebate is then worked to a good tight fit with the lid, the fit can be eased later. The whole of the inside can now be sanded and finished, including the lid rebate.

Fig. 386.   With the base completely finished on the inside it can be removed from the chuck. The lid can now be mounted using the smallest of the mini-collets, 19mm (¾in). I wish the makers would produce a smaller one. The fixing is not too robust as the grip is only 2mm (³⁄₃₂in) or so deep, therefore a 6mm (¼in) gouge is quite big enough and only very light cuts are taken.

Fig. 387.   In close-up using a HSS gouge completely on its side and keeping the cut to the right, or the lower half of the crescent shape of the tool cutting edge. Leave a small upstand in the middle of the work as this will strengthen the work, reducing it as you work inwards.

Fig. 388.   Use either calipers or your fingers to check the wall thickness as you work. Note the raised centre still supporting and, of course, giving that extra bit of strength to overcome the force of the mini-collet. The nature of its *expanding* type grip, will have a tendency to split the work, especially if over-tightened, or the work is turned very thinly.

Fig. 389.   With the inside of the lid finished it can be sanded and polished. Do not remove it from the chuck.

Fig. 390.   The base removed from the split ring fixing will still contain the original centering marks from the drive centre that was used to work the stuff for the ring. This centre mark can now be used to locate the base for final working to shape, utilising the section that was in the 6-in-1 to form the base or stand, and the box is sanded and finished. The tailstock is now withdrawn, and the base of the box can be sanded and polished if required. Remove the base and ease the fit for the lid using abrasive paper on the rebate of the lid which is still held in the mini-collet. This way there is no waste at all, what is more it is never necessary to work towards the large chuck or in the confined space between the work and the chuck/headstock. A knob is worked to complement the design of the box and the mini-collet hole used to effect its fitting.

Sand-glasses

Making sand-glasses calls for concentration, precision and a delicate touch. As the ends get regularly inverted in use they are liable to become scuffed. I like to vary the method by way of setting the frame of the sand-glass either in a base that's felt lined, or to swivel or hang. I am sure there are many other ways of producing a more interesting finished product than just three columns and two rounded ends. Care should be taken to select the timber, especially if it is highly figured, and in the design of the columns. The glass on the left of Fig. 391 is quite wrong, the columns are too large in the middle, the feet are too small to balance the size of the columns, and the strong grain effect makes it visually out of balance unless viewed from straight on. The sand-glass to the right, in my opinion, is just about right. Both use the same size glass and the left-hand one is kingwood, the right, blackwood.

The following description shows the method used to make a swivel sand-glass in a stand. The method is, of course, adaptable to make a variety of designs including those illustrated in Fig. 392.

Fig. 393.   Make a start with the columns first. While the
stuff can be set up between centres, I am using one of the
Coronet pin mandrels as used in the pepper mills section. It
has a hollow centre which also tapers, so that the work can
be removed as many times as you wish and will always be
replaced in the same position. This is an advantage,
especially to beginners, and we will see why in a moment.
Cross mark the stuff one end only, insert the other end into
the pin chuck, bring up the tailstock and apply light
pressure, just enough for the pin chuck to grip. I am using
a live centre to locate on the cross mark.

Fig. 394.   Work down to a cylinder, mark the shoulders at
each end with a skew and work two end dowels. Now
complete the detail in the centre of the column and while
there is plenty of thickness to support the work and lessen
whip, sand and finish. It is at this stage that some folk like
to remove the stuff and repeat the process for the remaining
columns and I think this is a good idea for repetition work
as each section of the design can be completed without
further shaping complicating the process. This shows the
advantage of the pin chuck.

Fig. 395.   Alternatively complete the design of the first
column and use it as a template for setting out the
dimensions of the others, completing them by eye.

Fig. 396.   For precision the profile gauge can be used,
both to lay off the dimensions and, as it is a true duplicate
of the first column, to complete the others. It is essential
that a locating point be established between the template
and the work, I am lining the left-hand end of the template
pins with the outer end of the chuck, and each piece of
work will be marked out and checked as work progresses
with the template in this position. The columns are set in
the base with the sand-glass using the same method as used
for the swivel sand-glass on the left of Fig. 392.

Fig. 397.   One of the swivel sand-glass frame ends set up in a screw chuck, it can be drilled right through. The desired shape is worked with a rebate for the mini-collet. The whole of this part can now be finished and polished.

Fig. 398.   There is a commercially made indexing plate and drilling jig, and we will discuss this in a moment. This is the sort of accessory that can be home-made, provided great care is taken in its preparation as it must be accurate and access to welding equipment is necessary. To start with I made a drilling jig from a short length of steel 19mm ($\frac{3}{4}$in) wide by 10mm ($\frac{3}{8}$in) thick and welded this to a length of 16mm ($\frac{5}{8}$in) diameter rod that fits my banjo (tool rest holder) at its lowest setting in the banjo i.e. with the square section steel resting on the banjo. All was locked up tight, a drill chuck containing a 6mm ($\frac{1}{4}$in) drill was set up in the headstock and my jig was pushed gently on to the drill to produce a hole which when offered at any angle to any work, would be dead on the centre line of the lathe. I made a further refinement by working a 8mm ($\frac{5}{16}$in) diameter hole below, as shown, and to centre this at any time all that is necessary is to proceed as in this Fig, but with a 8mm ($\frac{5}{16}$in) diameter drill fitted in the hole and a hose clip as a depth stop fitted and tightened as in Fig. 415. The jig can, of course, be made up in hardwood but it would not be as accurate, and certainly not as long lasting.

Fig. 399.   The indexing plate can also be home-made. I found a square of steel and with some difficulty, with the aid of a hacksaw, produced a reasonable disc. My local garage worked the central hole, and I divided the disc up into separate rings of 16, 8, 3, and 4 holes. All but the 3 holes are divisable into 16. Different lathes will vary, of course, but I lock this one with a bar from the riving knife support on my Coronet. With the work reversed and set up in the mini-collet chuck the inside of the frame end is worked. Position the work to bring the best of the grain to the front, get the best effect of colour and avoid any knots so that the holes will be where they are wanted and not at random. Satisfied that the work is correctly positioned the indexing head can now be locked, both on the spindle and the locking arm, and then all is fixed firm for drilling.

Fig. 400.   A rule is used to ensure the drilling jig will produce a hole square with the work, all is then locked up tight. I am using the 8mm ($\frac{5}{16}$in) diameter hole so the jig is positioned as described in Fig. 398 and supported with the hose clip.

Fig. 401.   As the jig is locked and the work is locked, insert the drill to contact. The depth of drilling can be measured at the rear of the jig and marked with tape. With the first hole completed the indexing plate can be released and repositioned for the next hole in the indexing plate to be selected and locked.

Fig. 402.   The holes for the columns completed. As the sand-glasses have caps on the ends, a hole to receive these ends can now be produced. The insides can now be finally sanded and polished and removed from the lathe.

Fig. 403.   The drilling for the pivot holes in the columns can either be worked once the stuff is reduced to a cylinder, or when the centre detail is completed. The work is set up here with a drive centre and a live centre of different pattern. It is best to mark the centre of the workpiece, complete the drilling on both columns without moving the drilling jig, and take the top and bottom shoulder dimensions from this centre line, this will ensure both pivot holes are equal in height.

Fig. 404.   With the two columns completed, set up a short length in a screw chuck and work the locking pin.

Fig. 405.   Then with the remainder of the stuff in the screw chuck, work the two buttons that will be required to fill the holes worked to accommodate the mini-collet chuck in the frame ends.

Fig. 406.   The two posts that will support the sand-glass frame, and upon which it will pivot, are made up in the same way as the frame columns and the pivot holes are drilled in the identical sequence. One column, the one without the locking pin, can be worked to a finish in one mounting, making good use of the vernier for marking.

Fig. 407.   The drill jig can be squared with the work by setting it tight against an accurately worked cylinder. As this hole will be produced right through the work, the tool rest is set behind the work with a length of waste stuff to prevent spelching, set tight between the rest and the post. This will also take up the thrust of the drill pressure.

Fig. 408.   With the two most important points, the pivot hole and the dowel shoulder completed, the rest of the detail can be worked.

Fig. 409.   The live post, the one that will contain the locking pin, is marked out, the pivot hole drilled and the shoulder worked. It is, of course, shorter, and the dowel provides the means of re-setting the work in the collet chuck to facilitate the drilling of the hole to accept the pivot locking pin.

Fig. 410.   The pivot pin, made in the same way as in Fig. 404, is inserted and held in position by tape. A hole is drilled right through, and approximately 6mm ($\frac{1}{4}$in) into the post. The pivot pin can now be removed, the pivot locking pin replaced and the whole turned to a finish as in Fig. 408.

Fig. 411.   The frame must be assembled with the pivot holes in line with the axis of pivot, this is best done by placing two drills or dowels in the holes and making up a jig as shown. It can be any shape so long as it clears any detail on the column and the edge is true. Adhesive is applied to the dowels on the columns, the frame ends are placed in position.

Fig. 412.   As long as the drills are firm in the holes and you work quickly, the straightedge will ensure the assembly will be true.

Fig. 413.   The bench vice or similar is used to hold all in position whilst the adhesive sets. If you have the shoulder sizes wrong, this is where you will require a few spare glasses, and a tight hold on your temper! Insert the sand-glass in the frame and insert the two buttons to cover the expanding collet chuck fixing. Leave the frame assembly to cure for several days.

Fig. 414.   To complete the rest of the assembly the posts are fitted into a previously made base with a dowel through the holes to ensure they are true with each other. When the adhesive has set the two can be assembled by placing adhesive in the holes in the columns only. The pivot pins are then located, the pivot locking pin is inserted, and the frame lined up and down and left to cure. There is a difference between adhesive setting and curing, i.e. Araldite will set in a few hours, it will not cure or reach its full strength as an adhesive for a period of seven days. This is a large glass and I find that without the locking pin when the glass is inverted with the sand in the top its weight, being top heavy, tends to bring it down. For smaller sand-glasses the locking pin is not strictly necessary, but fun to make nevertheless.

Fig. 415. The professionally-made indexing disc and drilling jig. The numerals are my idea, and rub on figures were used, covered with a lick of varnish to protect, I find this helps in dividing. The drilling jig, complete with hoseclip (not supplied) has its own $\frac{3}{4}$in hole into which can be set provision for $\frac{1}{4}$in, $\frac{3}{8}$in and $\frac{1}{2}$in drill guides. There are no metric equivalents at present. Available from Craft Supplies, Buxton, Derbyshire, England.

Fig. 416. The commercial indexing plate fits on the lathe in a different place to my home-made one, i.e. on the spindle, and is held in place by the chuck in use. Fortuitously my lathe has a threaded hole on a flat at the rear of the headstock, so it was a simple matter to make up a stop in a short length of angle iron, I expect Coronet owners will have been wondering what the banjo screw was doing in the photographs. There is another part that can be purchased to facilitate locking but different makes of lathe will require various ways of implementing its fitting.

Fig. 417. My method of locking the indexing or dividing head. Apart from the uses discussed, if your lathe does not have a facility for locking, this is but one more advantage, i.e. if you aspire to do a little carving or engraving on your turned work, steadying for sanding with the grain, etc.

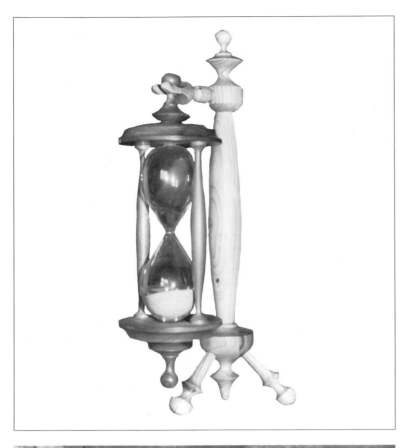

Fig. 418.   The hanging style is very popular, it's nice to know that there are a few folk who are as daft as I am.

Fig. 419.   Let us start by making the hook. This is prepared in the same way as the violin key type screw for the nutcrackers, Fig. 259–262, but with the addition of a hole through the centre of the flat. Careful marking prior to drilling is important. The prepared blank is set up, and here I am using the precision spigot chuck, but screw or collet will do just as well. With the shape formed one of the almost flat sides can be completely flattened and shaped. This will become the lower side when assembled. The other almost flat side is left as is, as this will take the knob when assembled.

Fig. 420.   Now we can turn to the column of the tripod stand. A length of approximately 50mm (2in) square stuff is mounted between centres, worked down to a cylinder and the fitting for the precision spigot chuck completed. It is worth going to this trouble as it will help when finishing off the top of the column, but again, a screw chuck or whatever will suffice. Another alternative will be discussed when we come to the top.

Fig. 421.   Finish shaping the column. I am using a length of English yew which is a delightful timber to work. A shape like this calls for a lot of waste. Put it to good use and practise with a few different tools to see how the timber reacts.

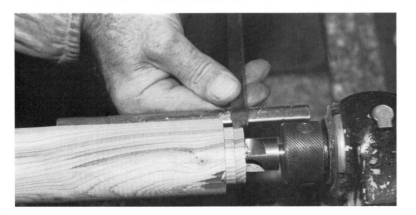

Fig. 422.   I have made several hanging sand-glasses over the years, but this new design idea was an attempt to produce a stand that would be an enlarged version of the style of the frame, looking at the finished product. I had to experiment to see if the stand would balance and when I make any more I will thin down the column of the stand a little more.

With the two ends in the rough shape it was time to drill the hole for the hook. Look at the stuff and bring the best feature of the grain to what will be the front of the stand, I have marked it with an X.

Fig. 423.   The gibbet hole is drilled with the jig pressed hard against the square section of the work. It could be angled up a little for better effect, and could open up a few other ways of hanging the frame.

Fig. 424.   In the same way the three holes for the tripod are completed to the desired angle.

Fig. 425.   Three neat, accurate and identical holes must be drilled at an angle and to a pre-determined depth. If there is any error the stand will wobble and you will have a lot of trimming to do when the feet are fitted. This is, to say the least, tricky, but with some form of jig, the job is much simplified. With the drilling complete the rest of the turning can be completed to the desired style. The feet can be made in the same way as described making cob holders, page 58. They must be of identical length so that when fixed with adhesive in identical holes the stand will be perfectly perpendicular.

Eggs and egg cups

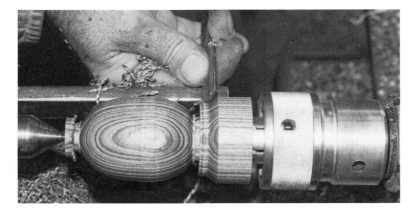

Fig. 426.   From left to right. Egg and cup in hornbeam; kingwood; in the bowl, ebony, cocobolo, saffron wood and lilac; Israeli olive egg in chestnut cup.

Fig. 427.   The kingwood that I have selected for making a small egg-shaped box is rare, expensive and I only have a little stock. This miniature work uses a different method from that described on page 115 with a different sequence and chucking. For this reason I decided to use the spigot chuck, intended basically for bowl making but eminently suitable for this work occasioning the minimum of waste. Arrowed is the 3mm ($\frac{1}{8}$in) long spigot, all that is necessary to hold the work. In addition to the method shown of finishing off, the technique described in making scoops could be used and means that only 3mm ($\frac{1}{8}$in) would be required.

Fig. 428.   With the stuff mounted in the precision spigot chuck and supported by the tailstock, work the rough shape of the egg plus, at the tailstock end, a further fitting for the chuck. Note that the grip of the chuck is a form of dovetail, in softish timbers this can be ignored, as even with the light tightening pressure required, in fact suggested by the makers, it will bite into the stuff and permit a perfect hold, in harder timbers, however, it is as well to work a similar shape to the grip of the chuck.

Fig. 429.   If the skew chisel is selected to finish the egg shape, set the rest about midway between centre line and the top of the work and this will avoid any undue angle of tool presentation. Use only the first 3mm ($\frac{1}{8}$in) of cutting edge from the short corner; this will prevent the tool catching and running uphill and will produce a very narrow shaving. If the shaving widens, lower the handle to stop cutting at once. Keep the speed to approximately 1500 rpm.

Fig. 430.   As you will be working on the inside of the lid do not remove too much at the tailstock at this stage. To avoid as much mis-match of grain as possible, take your narrowest parting tool and work the fitting flange for the lid, and then a parting cut right through to fell off, or as I have, almost through to be completed with a fine saw.

Fig. 431.   It is good practice to fell off with a saw as explained earlier on page 88. If resorting to a parting tool only, tailstock pressure must be released to prevent jamming, which would, in most cases, not only damage the rim of the lid, but also the true running of the stuff in the chuck.

Fig. 432.   The lid can be set safely aside while the base is worked. It will still be running dead true so the inside must be worked first while there is plenty to support it. Remove some of the waste with the spindle gouge, kept well on its side, taking light cuts. My little finger on the rest is used as a steady guide pivot.

Fig. 433.   Alternatively all, or the remainder, of the waste can be removed with a scraper to produce what is, in effect, an egg cup.

Fig. 434.   Before all the inside waste is removed, work the fitting flange for the lid, with the narrowest skew chisel available. Use only the long corner with the tool presented square to the work and horizontal. Take the lightest of cuts.

Fig. 435.   With the vernier set to the lid, the prongs will be a guide to work to almost a fit. The final fit is established with the lid itself, and must be very snug at this stage.

Fig. 436.   With the lid re-fitted the shape of the box can now be worked to a finish to whatever style is desired.

Fig. 437.   The base or stand can now be finished. Take only light cuts, using the spindle gouge completely on its side, and leave the final finishing of the base circumference to the last. Then if there is a slip with the gouge or parting tool there will be plenty of stuff left to remove the scars.

Fig. 438.   Make a preliminary cut for final parting off, but do not separate completely.

Fig. 439.   Still using the lid for support, the body can be sanded and polished, plus half of the lid if required.

Fig. 440.   The tailstock can now be withdrawn, the lid removed, and the inside of the box sanded and polished. This could, of course, have been completed after Fig. 435 or left as a final operation, but whenever it is done take care not to disturb the fit of the lid when sanding.

Fig. 441.   The base of the box can now be removed from the spigot chuck (unless you have two), and the lid fitted for hollowing. Use either a gouge in the same way as for the base, or a scraper.

Fig. 422.   Sand and polish the inside, and polish the fitting flange.

Fig. 443.   The thickness of the polish on the fitting flange may make the fit in the body over tight. If this happens it will be a simple matter to ease the flange in the base when re-mounting for final finishing.

Fig. 444.   Replace the base in the spigot chuck, re-fit the lid and bring up the tailstock to support. You may decide to use the spigot chuck waste to form a small knob, and for this type of box it could be a good idea. If the fit is perfect, with nothing to grip, the lid might be difficult to remove.

However, we will stick to the egg shape so reduce the waste end progressively in the form of a diminishing cone using alternate cuts with the gouge on its left side and then reversed.

Fig. 445.   Continue in this way taking only the lightest of cuts, allowing the bevel of the tool to run round the shape of the work, using it as a guide, and just lifting the bevel off slightly to effect the very fine cut. Remember that the inside of the lid is hollow, so don't get over enthusiastic. The marks left by the bevel of the tool rubbing the work can easily be removed with fine abrasive. For the courageous, a final gossamer cut all round with a skew, used as described in Fig. 429 will leave a super finish.

Fig. 446.   Finally finish with friction polish. The lid can, if necessary, be held on with one hand and a piece of rag, while polishing. Finally part off or, as described in

Fig. 353–358, you could make up a mandrel, reverse the box, part off and polish the base.

Fig. 447.   Making an egg-shaped box in this way is relatively easy as all, or nearly all the time you have an end to hold the work. To make an egg as such is not quite the same. With the stuff mounted up in the same way as before, the egg is worked to rough shape, eggs have a small end and a big end, real ones that is, so form the big end at the tailstock end and, working as before, let the shape formed guide the tool with fine gentle cuts.

Fig. 448.   With the big end completed, note the small pip still hanging on the tip of the live centre indicating a very light parting off cut. Withdraw the tailstock and completely sand and finish the egg from the tailstock end as far as the pencil line which is just past the thickest part of the workpiece.

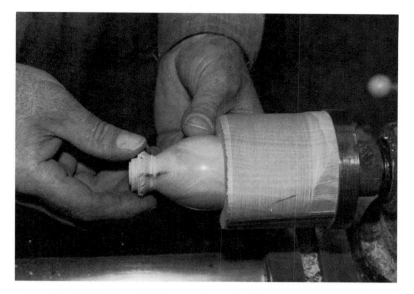

Fig. 449. In a spare screw chuck or small faceplate set up a piece of scrap softwood, grain running as shown in Fig. 263 and work a very slightly tapered, flat-bottomed cup mandrel, the taper being about one or two degrees. Do not sand but, by using the point of a very sharp skew after drilling out the worst of the waste, this will leave a surface that will grip, but not mark, the work.

Fig. 450. For things like eggs that come off the lathe completely finished, with no means of re-mounting, Danish oil is a good medium for finishing. However, we will for this exercise, polish this egg. To ensure the polish is not damaged by the mandrel four strips of self-adhesive felt can be inserted.

Fig. 451. Test for fit with the egg, it wants to enter the mandrel just past the widest or thickest part of the egg. If making several eggs from different size odds and ends, start with the smallest and work up, enlarging the mandrel as you go.

Fig. 452. As discussed before, work removed from the spigot or 6-in-1 chucks will have the original centre mark, locate this mark in the tailstock centre and use it to push the piece into the mandrel. This will give support for working and will ensure the work is running concentrically. Jammed thus in the mandrel, when the tailstock is removed, and if only the very lightest of pressure is used in finishing, the work will remain centred.

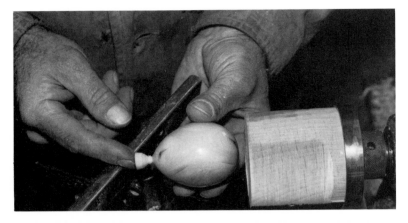

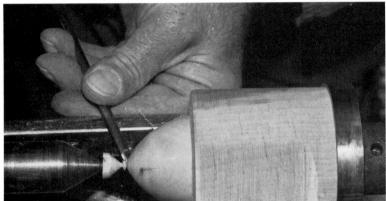

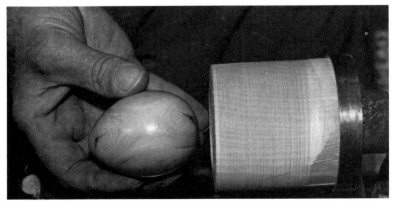

Fig. 453. It is sometimes difficult to judge a shape when only half or less than half of the work is seen. As long as you don't remove the pip containing the original centre the work can be removed from the housing, inspected, and replaced in the same position for further working/finishing.

Fig. 454. Replaced in the mandrel the small end is worked in the same way as in Fig. 445. The cone-shaped configuration is formed, gradually decreasing to a final push to sever the pip, using the gouge just rolled over a little more than completely on its side. While working the end it should be finished as far as the pencil mark shown in the next picture. Take care not to finish or sand right up to the edge of the housing as this will leave a mark.

Fig. 455. From the pencil mark to the end of the egg can now be sanded and polished, but to avoid dislodging the work only very gentle pressure must be used.

Fig. 456. The egg, polished all round and completely finished. The felt in the mandrel has prevented any damage to the surface. This egg is made from a piece of South African saffronwood (*Cassine papillosa*), it has a soft pink colour, very close grained, giving an almost ceramic look to it. As it was made from a small log, mounted off centre, the heart wood, with its deep purple slash gives an interesting and attractive look.

Lamps

Today there is such a vast selection of shades and accessories generally available one could go on forever and not make the same design or style twice. However, they all have one or two things in common. The flex must be taken through the stem and, preferably, out through the side, as opposed to underneath, and as this will be a project that will not only be in full view as a finished piece, but will also be illuminated, the finish is most important. Bearing these points in mind, the following pages describe making an oil-lamp style, from a log of yew, finished with a burnishable lacquer, hopping about, as we reach the finishing stages, between three different methods, or to be more accurate, effects and styles.

Fig. 457.   The log is mounted between centres, worked to a cylinder, and the two ends squared with a parting tool. The drive centre for work that is to be drilled right through is the same as normal, but has the provision of an extending spigot, this will facilitate re-location of the work for a progressive finishing process, guide the centre when it is used as a drill to counterbore the base, see Fig. 477, and is necessary to locate work that has, or will have, a hole bored through its length. A hole, in this case 8mm ($\frac{5}{16}$in) diameter must be produced to a depth of at least 38mm ($1\frac{1}{2}$in). If you have the facility of a drill press the deeper the better as this will save work from the other end later on. Note: as this is end grain take it slowly and withdraw the auger after every 25mm (1in) or so to clear the chips.

Fig. 458.   At the tailstock end I am using the revolving centre described in Fig. 202, fitted with a ring centre that is the same size as the long hole boring jig, Fig. 471–474. This will, of course, save lubrication in both working and in final finishing, and it is much more convenient to remount the work. A roughing out gouge can be used to remove the bulk of the waste quickly.

Fig. 459.   For tighter curves a spindle gouge of appropriate size might be found more convenient and will provide a clean finish.

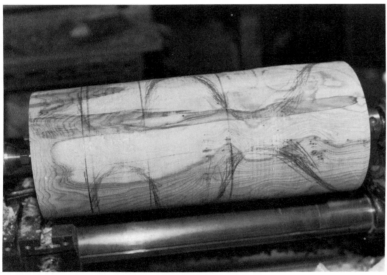

Fig. 460.   End grain is usually the most tedious to sand, and shapes like this one will have a lot of it. Take fine finishing cuts with a newly-honed gouge to prevent lungs full of dust and sore fingers. It is not always easy to see what a piece of timber will look like until you have worked into it a bit. As this was not an unduly attractive piece, I decided to leave it at this stage and start again on another piece that I had set aside some time ago. As you can see it is full of interest, character, and colour, not to mention several knots which will, I hope, demonstrate that timber with knots need not be daunting.

Fig. 461.   Mounted between centres as before. I had a rough idea as to what I wanted in the way of style, but rather than mark out some definite lines to work to, I sketched the intended shape on the stuff, which would enable me to vary the design to enhance any particular feature in the grain formation as and when it appeared.

Fig. 462.   The shade selected was, as are most oil lamps, in two parts, the chimney and the shade or diffuser, so a gallery must first be worked to accommodate these. Using a new diamond-shaped parting tool in HSS, to cut in approximately 25mm (1in) at a time, reduce the stuff at the tailstock end to this mark with a spindle gouge, and repeat as necessary.

Fig. 463.   Alternatively use a roughing-out gouge.

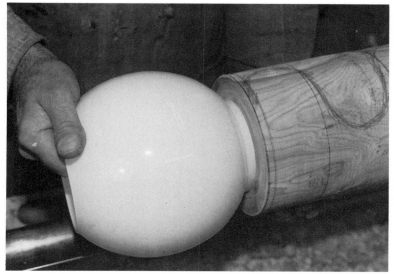

Fig. 464. Worked in this way it will be a simple matter to use calipers for the final sizing rather than try and gauge the width in a deep parting cut.

Fig. 465. The shade or diffuser housing is worked first and, working to a mark produced with calipers or vernier, lay a parting tool on its side and score the circle. This will prevent spelching.

Fig. 466. With a parting tool used semi-scraper fashion, but with the handle a little lower than horizontal, complete the housing to the required depth.

Fig. 467. Check for fit making it slightly loose to allow for any slight subsequent movement in the timber, and the thickness of finish used. Set the shade safely aside. The housing for the chimney is worked in the same way, either now, or if the diameter is of a size that the tailstock prevents working, it can be completed later when the workpiece is held secure in the long hole boring jig.

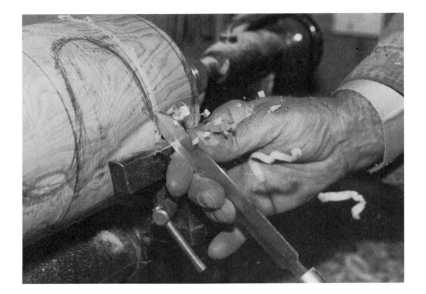

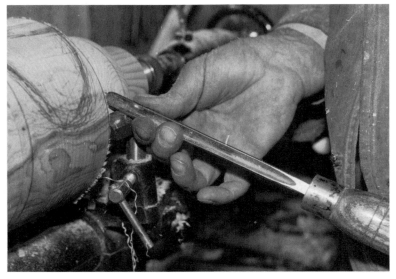

Fig. 468. Using a diamond-shaped parting tool to cut in and mark the basic shape. Do not cut too deep. The merits of this tool can be seen here. Unlike the conventional tool it is a uniform shape and thus usable over its entire length. I have found it is almost impossible to jam it, and being made in high speed steel the honed edge lasts and lasts.

Fig. 469. A combination of parting tool cuts, followed by shaping cuts from a spindle gouge, will quickly reveal the character of the stuff as the shape is formed. By taking it slowly it is now that any alterations of shape or style should be considered.

Fig. 470. The only alteration necessary for this project was to shorten it slightly. The design was being copied, with slight variations, from a lamp I had seen and liked, and that bit of waste was intended to permit me to slide the design a little in either direction should it prove necessary. Before the finishing cuts are made at the base, use the drilling jig to produce a 6mm ($\frac{1}{4}$in) hole for the flex to exit from the side of the base. I feel this is preferable to a slot across the base, with the problem of keeping the flex in it when it is in use.

Fig. 471. The method of setting work for long hole boring will vary slightly from lathe to lathe; the principle is, however, the same. For my machine I proceed as follows. Removing whatever tailstock centre has been used the long hole boring jig is set in a banjo tool rest holder and the centre of the jig is located in the mark left by the original centre. Thus the workpiece is returned perfectly centred.

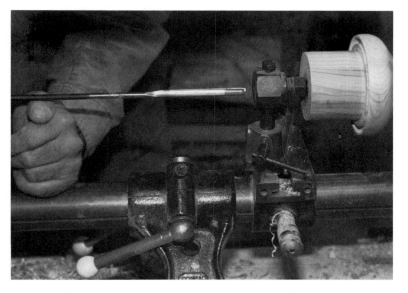

Fig. 472. The saddle (lathe bed slide) can now be brought up, the banjo located, and the boring jig can be slide along the centre to locate in the marks left by the ring centre. In the following order tighten the saddle, the banjo to the saddle, and then the jig to the banjo. The tailstock containing the dead centre can now be removed or, if necessary, with the dead centre removed, can be used to give a gentle push (with the saddle loosened) to tighten the work between centres.

Fig. 473. Alternatively, if you have the facility, slack off the lock nut on the top of the boring jig and tighten the work with a spanner, making sure to re-tighten the lock nut and to apply a spot of linseed oil for lubrication. As with normal work it is not necessary to overtighten.

Fig. 474. The long hole boring auger will now pass through the jig and into the work guided by the hole, which in this case is 8mm ($\frac{5}{16}$in). A straight hole can be produced up to the length of the auger, usually about 76cm (30in).

Fig. 475. Only the first 100mm (4in) of the auger will be guided by the jig after which the hole formed will be the guide. The auger is waisted to prevent binding in the bore hole. Gentle pressure is required, boring only 25mm (1in) or so and removing the auger to clear the chips. There is no common denominator as regards speed, this will vary to some extent with the timber used, and certainly never faster than 1000 rpm. If in doubt, start at the slowest speed and increase as necessary. Breakthrough will be felt, or can be measured by taping the auger. Take care not to foul the spigot on the drive centre.

Fig. 476.   With the boring completed the base can be counter-bored, in this instance I also had to remove the waste piece. By parting down to a diameter slightly smaller than the diameter of the drive centre, and having returned the tailstock end to the revolving cup centre, by slacking off the tailstock and allowing the work to revolve on the spigot, the lathe could be started at a slow speed and the workpiece held stationary by hand, the tailstock was then advanced and the drive centre cum counterbore tool, guided into the work by the spigot, was able to perform its function. Thus the waste piece was neatly removed and the drive centre continued, still guided by the spigot into the finished base to provide the counterbore necessary to permit the flex to be fitted and turned out through the side.

Fig. 477.   Using the drive centre as a counterbore tool, ensure the workpiece is revolving free on the spigot at a speed of 1000 rpm or less. Never faster. Hold the work with one hand, pushing it on to the centre by means of the tailstock advance wheel.

Fig. 478.   Sanded and sealed with a coat of clear lacquer thinned with approximately 25% thinners.

Fillers and finishing

There are several proprietory stoppers available, and the makers' instructions will come with the product. Over the years, however, I have found the most convenient, and permanent means of filling defects is epoxy (Araldite). For coloured work the mix can be thickened with fine sanding dust of any timber, or for polished articles, matched to the timber in use with poster paint. Whilst a perfect match is seldom necessary, after all few woods are exactly the same colour or shade right across the grain, with practice, almost invisible repairs can be made. This type of filler is non-shrinking and has considerable mechanical strength as well. It is simple to use, just mix the resin with the catalyst (hardener) in the usual way, then add dust or colour powder to thicken and produce the desired effect. When set, preferably overnight even for the fast set type, it can be worked with tools, sanded, and no finish that I know of will soften it once set.

Space will not permit coverage in depth on the subject of finishing, so I will conclude by describing one or two products that I find suitable for the turner.

Danish oil is a simple and easy to use product. The oil is applied with a brush or cloth, left for ten minutes, wiped dry and left for four to eight hours. Repeat this four or five times and then leave for two or three days to harden before polishing to a dull sheen, either on the lathe at about 500 rpm, or by hand with a soft cloth. This finish will be found very durable and normal maintenance with household polishes will be all that is required.

For a high gloss I use a catalyst activated lacquer. There are several makes but for the purpose of discussion I have

used Rustins Plastic Coating which is available as a clear varnish or in black or white. Full instructions for mixing come with the product, so I will only add that I have found, on the recommendation of the makers, that for lathe polishing approximately 10% extra catalyst (hardener) should be used. This makes the mix a little harder but does not seem to reduce its pot life.

Fig. 479.   The first and perhaps the most important aspect in producing any kind of super finish is to start with a perfect surface. Any slight imperfections that you hope will be covered by the product used will manifest themselves, and the smoother and more highly polished the surface the more obvious will any sanding rings, chips, or cracks become. For this reason a very critical examination must be made when sanding and any cracks or shakes must be filled before a further sanding, reducing to at least 350 grit garnet or similar. Satisfied that you are ready to apply the finish, in this case white plastic, the surface can either be covered with a thinned (by 25% of thinners) coat of the colour, or clear lacquer of the same product. Then, when dry in approximately 1–2 hours, a further coat of unthinned mix. Allow a further 2–3 hours at approximately 21°C (70°F) and with 600 grade wet and dry used wet, and taking great care not to sand through the coating especially on those sharp edges, flat the surface. This will show how good your sanding was as any imperfections will now be seen. A similar effect can be obtained by dispensing with the first coat of thinned mix using grain filler instead. On coloured work this can certainly save at least two coats of colour, but for clear, lacquered work I prefer to fill the grain with lacquer, and on open grain timbers this can take several coats.

Satisfied that the surface is now ready to take the finishing process, a wipe with a tack rag to remove any particles of dust that might adhere to the work. A tack rag

is an adhesive duster available from good paint and colour merchants but if one is not available, a piece of clean rag moistened with white spirit will suffice.

Fig. 480.   The ideal place to effect the painting is away from the dust of the workshop. If this is not possible, at least clear the lathe and perhaps put a few moistened newspapers on the floor to prevent dust being raised by the movement of the feet. In truth it is almost impossible to eliminate dust nuisance but any steps that can be taken to minimise it will pay dividends. With the workpiece between centres, apply the finish in the normal way of painting, then, with just light pressure on the brush, lay off by holding the brush stationary, and revolving the work by means of the lathe pulleys.

Fig. 481.   How many coats to apply will depend very much on your skill in painting an even layer at each application, and how carefully you flatten each coat, certainly a minimum of two, and for me usually four or five. Successive coats can be applied at intervals of approximately one hour at a temperature of 21°C (70°F) and very lightly flatted with 600 grade wet and dry used wet, between coats as illustrated. Rubber gloves will protect the skin and prevent irritation.

Fig. 482.   The final coat should be flatted completely, and should have no shiny spots or runs. Stubborn shiny areas can be flatted with the lathe stopped to prevent the surrounding areas being flatted unnecessarily. Keep the speed of the lathe as slow as possible for all finishing – 350 rpm is ideal. If you do not have such a slow speed, compensate with a gossamer light touch.

Fig. 483.   The makers will indicate how to use the burnishing cream but I find it best to keep the cloth well moistened with water and by starting with heavy pressure, relaxing the pressure to a light touch as the matt surface becomes gloss. Keep the cloth moving all the time and stop frequently to inspect the work.

Fig. 484.   Finally buff with a soft cloth and a high gloss finish will be yours.

Fig. 485. A great deal of fun can be had with these finishes, especially if you have an artistic bent. Delightful antique effects can be obtained by actually sanding through on some of the high sections or profiles as this tends to give an old and well used look. By covering say a black article so treated with a few coats of satin finish clear lacquer, the entire article will be completely protected. The white finish looks particularly attractive left matt and not burnished. Finish with 1000 grade wet and dry used very wet and with a little soap, for the final flatting.

Fig. 486. There are basically two methods of fitting the bayonet bulb holder, for most applications I prefer the inserted nipple. The standard thread appears to be $\frac{3}{8}$in Whitworth, and this can be worked with a tap in the normal way. If a tap is not available, by cutting a slot across the base of the nipple to a depth of 6mm ($\frac{1}{4}$in), a thread of sorts can be worked in softish woods but beware of splitting. The alternative is the flanged type held with three screws.

Fig. 487. The spring clip required for some shades is fitted under the nipple. If in the slightest doubt about the wiring of the bulb holder please consult a qualified electrician. Any article that is to be 'electrified' and handled is a potential danger to the user, I know you will be busting to use your lamp, but consideration of safety could save a life.

Fig. 488. Apart from being used as an electric lamp this style of shade can be most effective as a candle holder.

Index